M
$26.20

EVANSTON PUBLIC LIBRARY

P9-CAL-686

345.02 Writing
The Patriot Act /

FEB 0 6 2007

345.02
writing

Writing the Critical Essay

THE PATRIOT ACT

An OPPOSING VIEWPOINTS® Guide

Lauri S. Friedman, *Book Editor*

Bonnie Szumski, *Publisher, Series Editor*
Helen Cothran, *Managing Editor*

OPPOSING
VIEWPOINTS®
SERIES

GREENHAVEN PRESS

An imprint of Thomson Gale, a part of The Thomson Corporation

THOMSON
— ✦ —
GALE

EVANSTON PUBLIC LIBRARY
1703 ORRINGTON AVENUE
EVANSTON, ILLINOIS 60201

Detroit • New York • San ... ...aine • London • Munich

© 2006 Thomson Gale, a part of The Thomson Corporation.

Thomson and Star Logo are trademarks and Gale and Greenhaven Press are registered trademarks used herein under license.

For more information, contact
Greenhaven Press
27500 Drake Rd.
Farmington Hills, MI 48331-3535
Or you can visit our Internet site at http://www.gale.com

ALL RIGHTS RESERVED.
No part of this work covered by the copyright hereon may be reproduced or used in any form or by any means—graphic, electronic, or mechanical, including photocopying, recording, taping, Web distribution or information storage retrieval systems—without the written permission of the publisher.

Articles in Greenhaven Press anthologies are often edited for length to meet page requirements. In addition, original titles of these works are changed to clearly present the main thesis and to explicitly indicate the author's opinion. Every effort is made to ensure that Greenhaven Press accurately reflects the original intent of the authors.

Every effort has been made to trace the owners of copyrighted material.

LIBRARY OF CONGRESS CATALOGING-IN-PUBLICATION DATA

The Patriot Act / Lauri S. Friedman, book editor.
   p. cm. — (Writing the critical essay)
  Includes bibliographical references and index.
  ISBN 0-7377-3525-2 (lib. : alk. paper)
  1. United States. Uniting and Strengthening America by Providing Appropriate Tools Required to Intercept and Obstruct Terrorism (USA PATRIOT ACT) Act of 2001. 2. Terrorism—Prevention—United States. 3. Critical thinking—Problems, exercises, etc. 4. Essay—Authorship—Problems, exercises, etc. 5. Rhetoric—Problems, exercises, etc. I. Friedman, Lauri S. II. Series.
  KF9430.Z9P38 2006
  345.73'02—dc22
                                       2005055072

Printed in the United States of America

Foreword   5

Introduction   7
Background to Controversy: The Patriot Act and
American Society

**Section One: Opposing Viewpoints on the
Patriot Act**

Viewpoint One: The Patriot Act Fights Terrorism   13
Paul Rosenzweig

Viewpoint Two: The Patriot Act Does Not Fight
Terrorism   19
Bob Barr

Viewpoint Three: The Patriot Act Reduces Freedom   24
Al Gore

Viewpoint Four: The Patriot Act Does Not Reduce
Freedom   30
James D. Zirin

Viewpoint Five: The Patriot Act Unfairly Targets
Immigrants   36
David Cole

Viewpoint Six: The Patriot Act Does Not Target
Immigrants   41
Michelle Malkin

Section Two: Model Essays and Writing Exercises

Preface A: The Five-Paragraph Essay   48

Preface B: The Expository Essay   50

Essay One: America's Controversy: The Patriot Act   52
    Exercise A: Create an Outline from an Existing Essay   56

Essay Two: The Patriot Act Is a Necessary Law
Enforcement Tool   58
    Exercise A: Create an Outline from an Existing Essay   62
    Exercise B: Create an Outline for an Opposing
           Expository Essay   62

Essay Three: Looking and Listening: The Patriot Act's
Power to Monitor   64
    Exercise A: Examining Introductions and
           Conclusions   69
    Exercise B: Using Quotations to Enliven Your Essay   71

Final Writing Challenge: Write Your Own Expository
Five-Paragraph Essay   72

Section Three: Supporting Research Material
    Appendix A: Facts About the Patriot Act   77

    Appendix B: Finding and Using Sources of
    Information   81

    Appendix C: Using MLA Style to Create a
    Works Cited List   85

    Appendix D: Sample Essay Topics   87

    Organizations to Contact   88

    Bibliography   91

    Index   94

    Picture Credits   96

    About the Editor   96

Examining the state of writing and how it is taught in the United States was the official purpose of the National Commission on Writing in America's Schools and Colleges. The commission, made up of teachers, school administrators, business leaders, and college and university presidents, released its first report in 2003. "Despite the best efforts of many educators," commissioners argued, "writing has not received the full attention it deserves." Among the findings of the commission was that most fourth-grade students spent less than three hours a week writing, that three-quarters of high school seniors never receive a writing assignment in their history or social studies classes, and that more than 50 percent of first-year students in college have problems writing error-free papers. The commission called for a "cultural sea change" that would increase the emphasis on writing for both elementary and secondary schools. These conclusions have made some educators realize that writing must be emphasized in the curriculum. As colleges are demanding an ever-higher level of writing proficiency from incoming students, schools must respond by making students more competent writers. In response to these concerns, the SAT, an influential standardized test used for college admissions, required an essay for the first time in 2005.

Books in the Writing the Critical Essay: An Opposing Viewpoints Guide series use the patented Opposing Viewpoints format to help students learn to organize ideas and arguments and to write essays using common critical writing techniques. Each book in the series focuses on a particular type of essay writing—including expository, persuasive, descriptive, and narrative—that students learn while being taught both the five-paragraph essay as well as longer pieces of writing that have an opinionated focus. These guides include everything necessary to help students research, outline, draft, edit, and ultimately write successful essays across the curriculum, including essays for the SAT.

Using Opposing Viewpoints

This series is inspired by and builds upon Greenhaven Press's acclaimed Opposing Viewpoints series. As in the parent series, each book in the Writing the Critical Essay series focuses on a timely and controversial social issue that provides lots of opportunities for creating thought-provoking essays. The first section of each volume begins with a brief introductory essay that provides context for the opposing viewpoints that follow. These articles are chosen for their accessibility and clearly stated views. The thesis of each article is made explicit in the article's title and is accentuated by its pairing with an opposing or alternative view. These essays are both models of persuasive writing techniques and valuable research material that students can mine to write their own informed essays. Guided reading and discussion questions help lead students to key ideas and writing techniques presented in the selections.

The second section of each book begins with a preface discussing the format of the essays and examining characteristics of the featured essay type. Model five-paragraph and longer essays then demonstrate that essay type. The essays are annotated so that key writing elements and techniques are pointed out to the student. Sequential, step-by-step exercises help students construct and refine thesis statements; organize material into outlines; analyze and try out writing techniques; write transitions, introductions, and conclusions; and incorporate quotations and other researched material. Ultimately, students construct their own compositions using the designated essay type.

The third section of each volume provides additional research material and writing prompts to help the student. Additional facts about the topic of the book serve as a convenient source of supporting material for essays. Other features help students go beyond the book for their research. Like other Greenhaven Press books, each book in the Writing the Critical Essay series includes bibliographic listings of relevant periodical articles, books, Web sites, and organizations to contact.

Writing the Critical Essay: An Opposing Viewpoints Guide will help students master essay techniques that can be used in any discipline.

Background to Controversy: The Patriot Act and American Society

T he USA Patriot Act is among the most important and controversial American laws. It is also so complex that it can be difficult to grasp what it is really all about. The act is 342 pages long and contains over a hundred separate provisions, many of which are written in cumbersome legal language that is hard for the average American to understand. This lack of understanding is one reason why arguments over the Patriot Act tend to generate more controversy than clarity. But at the heart of the debate over whether the act is hurting or helping American society is a fairly simple question: In what kind of society do Americans want to live?

It came as a terrible shock to most Americans to learn that the nineteen hijackers involved in the terrorist attacks of September 11, 2001, had lived in the United States while plotting to take American lives. The hijackers had fooled virtually everyone—they lived in average houses in average neighborhoods, attended schools, and held jobs. That the terrorists were able to so thoroughly blend into American society was viewed as a serious weakness in national security. A frightened public, legislators, and law enforcement authorities concluded that if homicidal terrorists could successfully pass themselves off as ordinary citizens, then no ordinary citizen could be automatically ruled out as harmless. It meant that everyone needed to be watched more closely. The Patriot Act was drafted and passed in the immediate aftermath of September 11, therefore, to improve law enforcement agencies' surveillance capabilities to catch suspected terrorists.

But historically, Americans have fiercely protected themselves against government intrusion. Objections to the Patriot Act soon surfaced. Many people have voiced concern that under the guise of helping authorities catch terrorists, portions of the Patriot Act threaten individual freedoms such as the right to privacy and the basic legal principle that a person is innocent until proven guilty. Under the new act, they argue, simple, innocent—and private—activities such as becoming scuba certified, applying to attend school, joining a particular political organization, or checking out a certain category of library book could place a person on a government watch list.

Twin beams of light commemorate the World Trade Center towers, destroyed in the September 11, 2001, terrorist attacks. The Patriot Act was passed immediately following the attacks.

Senator Russell Feingold (D-WI) spoke for many concerned Americans when he complained that the act's sweeping provisions threatened to erode the very foundations upon which the United States was built. As he cast the lone dissenting vote in the Senate against the Patriot Act, he said, "Preserving our freedom is one of the main reasons that we are now engaged in this new war on terrorism. We will lose that war without firing a shot if we sacrifice the liberties of the American people."[1]

Yet, it seems increasingly clear that concern for freedom needs to be balanced with the knowledge that living in a completely open society makes Americans vulnerable. Terrorists have proved they can blend into American society, so it seems only sensible to strengthen defenses that can expose them, catch them, and foil their plots. Many Americans have expressed their willingness to surrender a certain level of freedom or to tolerate modest intrusions on their privacy because they feel that being safe is worth it. Indeed, a July 2005 Fox News/Opinion

A protestor demonstrates his opinion that the Patriot Act threatens freedom.

Several provisions of the Patriot Act caused some Americans to question whether the act keeps the country safe without compromising liberty.

Dynamics Poll found that 64 percent of Americans were willing to give up some degree of personal freedom to reduce the threat of terrorism. The Patriot Act is thus seen by its supporters as a good weapon with which to protect the more important freedoms enjoyed by Americans, even if that means accepting government intrusion into their lives.

It is important to note that several of the Patriot Act's provisions are set to expire during 2006. Congress will then have to vote on whether these provisions should be permanently readopted, temporarily readopted, replaced by new provisions, or simply dropped. But if certain provisions of the Patriot Act are subject to change, the basic arguments surrounding its existence are not. The enduring questions about how American society should be shaped and how security and liberty should be balanced are sure to be relevant for a long time to come, just as they were integral to establishing a country that would, over time, so enthusiastically devote itself to the pursuit of freedom.

Long before the attacks of September 11 and the antiterrorism laws that followed, a great American warned his fellow citizens about the risks involved in seeking the right balance between freedom and safety. In 1759 Benjamin Franklin said, "They that can give up essential liberty to obtain a little temporary safety deserve neither liberty nor safety." [2] Deciding what freedoms constitute essential liberty and what actions might achieve lasting security are some of the many difficult tasks of the post–September 11 world. To this end, *Writing the Critical Essay: An Opposing Viewpoints Guide: The Patriot Act* exposes readers to the basic debates surrounding the nation's most controversial legislation and encourages them to develop their own opinions and writings on the matter.

Notes

1. Russell Feingold, address to the U.S. Senate, Washington, D.C., October 25, 2001.
2. Benjamin Franklin, *Historical Review of Pennsylvania,* 1759.

THE PATRIOT AC
IS NOT
PATRIOTIC ACTI

**Section One:
Opposing Viewpoints
on the Patriot Act**

The Patriot Act Fights Terrorism

Paul Rosenzweig

Paul Rosenzweig is a professor of law at George Mason University. In the following essay he argues that the Patriot Act helps law enforcement agencies fight terrorism. Rosenzweig explains that the Patriot Act helps officers dismantle terror cells in various parts of the country. It also has been useful in prosecuting suspected terrorists and allowing intelligence agencies to share information. Rosenzweig maintains that the Patriot Act is important for preventing another terrorist attack like September 11, 2001.

Consider the following questions:

1. According to the author, the Patriot Act helped dismantle terror cells in what three American states?
2. Who is Enaam Arnaout, according to Rosenzweig?
3. According to the author, in what way does the U.S. government have a "dual obligation" to its citizens?

Falsehood, according to Mark Twain's famous dictum, gets halfway around the world before the truth even gets its shoes on. Time and again, outlandish stories seem to grow legs and find wide distribution before the truth can catch up.

A good example is the USA Patriot Act. It's so broadly demonized now, you'd never know it passed with overwhelming support in the days immediately after Sept. 11, 2001.

Paul Rosenzweig, "Face Facts: Patriot Act Aids Security, Not Abuse," *The Christian Science Monitor*, July 29, 2004, p. 9. Copyright © 2004 by The Christian Science Publishing Society. All rights reserved. Reproduced by permission of the author.

With senators looking on, President Bush signs the Patriot Act into law on October 26, 2001, forty-five days after the September 11 terrorist attacks.

Critics paint the Patriot Act as a caldron of abuse and a threat to civil liberties. Advocacy groups run ads depicting anonymous hands tearing up the Constitution and a tearful old man fearful to enter a bookstore. Prominent politicians who voted for the act call for a complete overhaul, if not outright repeal.

But the truth is catching up. And the first truth is that the Patriot Act was absolutely vital to protect America's security.

The Patriot Act Helps Catch Terrorists

Before 9/11, US law enforcement and intelligence agencies were limited by law in what information they could share with each other. The Patriot Act tore down that wall—and officials have praised the act's value.

As former Attorney General Janet Reno told the 9/11 commission, "Generally, everything that's been done in the Patriot Act has been helpful . . . while at the same time maintaining the balance with respect to civil liberties."

And as [former] Attorney General John Ashcroft's recent report to Congress makes clear, this change in the law has real, practical consequences. Information-sharing facilitated by the Patriot Act, for example, was critical to dismantling terror cells in Portland, Ore.; Lackawanna, N.Y.; and

Police confiscate property from a suspected terrorist in Detroit. The Patriot Act helps police make such seizures.

The Patriot Act helped law enforcement prosecute suspected terrorist Enaam Arnaout (left), who had connections with al Qaeda leader Osama bin Laden (above).

Virginia. Likewise the act's information-sharing provisions assisted the prosecution in San Diego of those involved with an Al Qaeda drugs-for-weapons plot involving "Stinger" antiaircraft missiles.

It also aided in the prosecution of Enaam Arnaout, who had a longstanding relationship with Osama bin Laden and who used his charity organization to obtain funds illicitly from unsuspecting Americans for terrorist groups and to serve as a channel for people to contribute knowingly to such groups.

These are not trivial successes. They're part of an enormous, ongoing effort to protect America from further terrorist attacks.

A Critical Antiterror Tool

We cannot, of course, say that the Patriot Act alone can stop terrorism. Every time we successfully use the new tools at our disposal to thwart a terrorist organization, that's a victory.

Yet remarkably, some of these vital provisions allowing the exchange of information between law enforcement and intelligence agencies will expire [in 2006]. So here's a second truth: If Congress does nothing, then parts of the law will return to where they were on the day before 9/11—to a time when our government couldn't, by law, connect all the dots. Nobody wants a return to those days, but that is where we are headed if Congress does not set aside its partisan debates. . . .

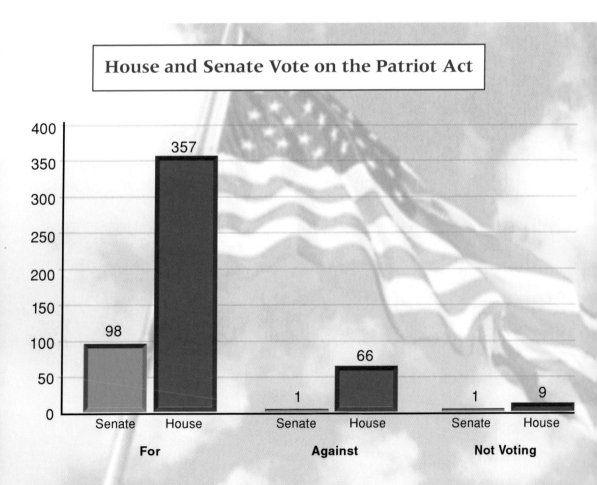

House and Senate Vote on the Patriot Act

Source: Department of Justice, *Preserving Life and Liberty*, 2004.

Government's obligation is a dual one: to provide security against violence and to preserve civil liberty. This is not a zero-sum game. We can achieve both goals if we empower government to do sensible things while exercising oversight to prevent any real abuses of authority. The Patriot Act, with its reasonable extension of authority to allow the government to act effectively with appropriate oversight rules, meets this goal.

And the truth eventually catches up to the fiction.

Analyze the essay:

1. The author frames his essay with a Mark Twain quote about truth and falsehood. In what way do you think this technique enhances the essay?

2. In this essay Rosenzweig explains why he believes the Patriot Act is a necessary tool for fighting terrorism. In the following essay Bob Barr explains why he believes the Patriot Act does not help fight terrorism. After reading both essays, with which author do you agree? What pieces of evidence helped you form your opinion?

The Patriot Act Does Not Fight Terrorism

Bob Barr

In the following essay author Bob Barr argues that the Patriot Act does not help law enforcement personnel fight terrorism. He contends that laws that existed prior to the Patriot Act were strong enough to fight terrorists—the problem is that they were not properly enforced. He accuses lawmakers of using the Patriot Act as an excuse to pass sweeping laws that threaten Americans' freedom. He concludes that the Patriot Act offers Americans no real extra security. Barr represented Georgia in the U.S. House of Representatives from 1995 to 2003.

Consider the following questions:

1. According to the author, what pre–Patriot Act laws did the September 11 terrorists break?
2. Why does the author think it would have been appropriate for federal officials to apologize to Americans after the September 11 terrorist attacks?
3. What do you think Barr means when he refers to the Patriot Act as a "legislative grab bag"?

The USA Patriot Act of 2001 and the proposed Son of Patriot Act [that is, expanded Patriot Act laws, are] now being debated in the Congress at the request of the Bush administration.

These are frightening laws. Left unchecked, they threaten the constitutional basis on which our society is premised:

Bob Barr, "Patriot Act Games: It Can Happen Here," *The American Spectator*, August 19, 2003. Copyright © 2003 by *The American Spectator*. Reproduced by permission.

Wasserman. © 2001 by *The Boston Globe*. Reproduced by permission of Tribune Media Services.

that citizens possess rights over their persons and property and that they retain those rights unless there is a sound, articulated, and specific reason for the government to take them away (i.e., probable cause of criminal activity). The Fourth Amendment's guarantee against unreasonable search and seizure will have been gutted.

Possibly the measures contained in the Patriot Act, its proposed new offspring, and numerous other official surveillance measures now in effect or being planned were, as we're told, essential responses to the terrorist attacks of September 11, 2001. Possibly they are specifically tailored to meet such threats in the future, and the best and most efficient way to minimize the likelihood of such attacks. Perhaps then one could accept some of the encroachments on civil liberties as necessary and perhaps even worthwhile. But they're not.

Pre–Patriot Act Laws Were Adequate

The terrorists who gained access to those four jetliners in the early morning of September 11, 2001, carried weapons that were already illegal on commercial aircraft. They were already in this country illegally, or had overstayed their lawful presence. Their pockets were stuffed with false identification. Their knowledge of the aircraft's performance and handling had been gathered in violation of federal law. Much of the information that could have alerted law enforcement officials to their horrendous plot was already within the possession of law enforcement and intelligence agencies. The government had sufficient lawful power to identify and stop the plotters. It failed to do so.

Yet what was the response to this tragedy? Did a single federal agency or official come before the American people and say: "We're sorry. We had the power to stop these terrorists. We had sufficient money to have done so. We simply made mistakes and errors in judgment, which will now be corrected." Not a chance.

Instead, what we saw—and I saw personally, as a member of both the House Judiciary Committee and the Government Reform Committee—was agency after agency, bureaucrat after bureaucrat come before us and say, "You [the Congress] didn't give us enough legal power or money to stop these attacks. We need more money. We need more power." But not wishing to appear soft on terrorism, the Congress—not surprisingly—gave them very nearly whatever they asked for.

The hijackers of American Airlines Flight 11 slipped through airport security with fake IDs and box cutters, items banned under pre–Patriot Act laws.

Mohamed Atta

Satam M. al Suqami

Abdulaziz Alomari

Waleed M. Alshehri

Wail M. Alshehri

Critics of the Patriot Act contend that it grants the government excessive power in the search for terrorists.

An Excuse to Grant Power

And what they asked for definitely was not narrowly tailored, limited, or designed only to correct those specific provisions of existing laws that needed to be tweaked. What the bureaucrats sought—and largely got—were far-reaching powers that applied not just to antiterrorism needs but to virtually *all* federal criminal laws. Changes to wiretapping laws, to search and seizures, easier access to tangible evidence—the list is long and complex. In essence, the attacks of September 11 provided an excuse for the executive branch to pull off the shelf, dust off, and push into law a whole series of proposals it had sought unsuccessfully for years.

Moreover, the direction Washington is now turning—making it easier to gather evidence on *everyone* within our borders, in an effort to develop profiles of terrorists and identify them amid the masses of data—is not likely to be particularly successful at thwarting terrorist attacks. As the CIA itself noted in an unclassified study reportedly conducted in 2001, terrorists typically take great pains to avoid being profiled: they don't want to get caught, and in fact it is essentially impossible to profile terrorists.

We Need Better Law *Enforcement,* Not Better Laws

The real way to catch terrorists is with better intelligence gathering, better coordination and analysis, better utilization of existing law enforcement tools, and quicker and more appropriate dissemination of that intelligence. The key word is *better*. With a few notable exceptions, the USA Patriot Act is a legislative grab bag that does little to encourage *better* law enforcement and intelligence work. Instead, we have an unprecedented expansion of federal law enforcement powers that significantly diminishes the civil liberties of American citizens, with only marginal increases in real security.

These fears are not, as some are saying, unfounded. And all I've done is scratch the surface of what is shaping up as a dramatic alteration to the very foundation of our society. The original Winston Smith [the character from George Orwell's dystopia, *1984*] was scared to death of the power of government—so we should be too. It was Benjamin Franklin, not George Orwell, who said, "They that give up essential liberty to obtain a little temporary safety deserve neither liberty nor safety." But, it could just as well have been.

Analyze the essay:
1. Barr discusses a study conducted by the CIA in 2001 which found that terrorists take great pains to avoid acting or looking the way one might generally expect terrorists to act or look. How does Barr use this information to support his argument?
2. As a former representative, Barr served on the Judiciary Committee and the Government Reform Committee, two groups involved with determining the country's laws, including the Patriot Act. Does knowing Barr's background as a government official influence your opinion of his argument in any way? Why or why not?

The Patriot Act Reduces Freedom

Al Gore

In the following speech delivered in Washington, D.C., former U.S. vice president Al Gore explains several ways in which he believes the Patriot Act reduces Americans' freedom. He argues that the legislation allows the government to intrude on the privacy of Americans and take away their constitutional rights. In other times of crisis, Gore argues, the government has restricted the rights and liberties of Americans only to later realize that such acts were unconstitutional. He recommends the Patriot Act be replaced with milder legislation that better protects the freedom of American citizens.

Consider the following questions:

1. According to Gore, how has the Patriot Act affected the way searches are carried out?
2. What does the author claim can happen to a person if he or she is determined to be an enemy combatant?
3. What kinds of records can the FBI demand access to, according to Gore?

I want to talk about . . . what has happened to civil liberties and security since the vicious attacks against America of September 11, 2001—and it's important to note at the outset that the Administration and the Congress have brought about many beneficial and needed improvements to make law enforcement and intelligence community efforts more effective against potential terrorists.

Al Gore, "Prepared Remarks on Freedom and Security," www.moveon.org, November 9, 2003.

But a lot of other changes have taken place that a lot of people don't know about and that come as unwelcome surprises.

A Loss of Inalienable Rights

For example, for the first time in our history, American citizens have been seized by the executive branch of government and put in prison without being charged with a crime, without having the right to a trial, without being able to see a lawyer, and without even being able to contact their families.

President Bush is claiming the unilateral right to do that to any American citizen he believes is an "enemy combatant." Those are the magic words. If the President alone

Former vice president Al Gore opposes the Patriot Act.

decides that those two words accurately describe some-one, then that person can be immediately locked up and held incommunicado for as long as the President wants, with no court having the right to determine whether the facts actually justify his imprisonment.

Now if the President makes a mistake, or is given faulty information by somebody working for him, and locks up the wrong person, then it's almost impossible for that person to prove his innocence—because he can't talk to a lawyer or his family or anyone else and he doesn't even have the right to know what specific crime he is accused of committing. So a constitutional right to liberty and the pursuit of happiness that we used to think of in an old-fashioned way as "inalienable" can now be instantly stripped from any American by the President with no meaningful review by any other branch of government.

How do we feel about that? Is that OK?

Wolverton. © 2005 by Monte Wolverton. Reproduced by permission of Cagle Cartoons.

Authority to Spy on the Public

Here's another recent change in our civil liberties: Now, if it wants to, the federal government has the right to monitor every website you go to on the internet, keep a list of everyone you send email to or receive email from and everyone whom you call on the telephone or who calls you—and they don't even have to show probable cause that you've done anything wrong. Nor do they ever have to report to any court on what they're doing with the information. Moreover, there are precious few safeguards to keep them from reading the content of all your email.

Everybody fine with that?

If so, what about this next change?

For America's first 212 years, it used to be that if the police wanted to search your house, they had to be able to convince an independent judge to give them a search warrant and then (with rare exceptions) they had to go bang on your door and yell, "Open up!" Then, if you didn't quickly open up, they could knock the door down. Also, if they seized anything, they had to leave a list explaining what they had taken. That way, if it was all a terrible mistake (as it sometimes is) you could go and get your stuff back.

But that's all changed now. Starting [in 2001] federal agents were given broad new statutory authority by the Patriot Act to "sneak and peek" in non-terrorism cases. They can secretly enter your home with no warning—whether you are there or not—and they can wait for months before telling you they were there. And it doesn't have to have any relationship to terrorism whatsoever. It applies to any garden-variety crime. And the new law makes it very easy to get around the need for a traditional warrant—simply by saying that searching your house might have some connection (even a remote one) to the investigation of some agent of a foreign power. Then they can go to another court, a secret court, that more or less has to give them a warrant whenever they ask. . . .

Protect Our Liberties

Preserving our freedom is one of the main reasons that we are now engaged in this new war on terrorism. We will lose that war without firing a shot if we sacrifice the liberties of the American people.

Russell Feingold, address to the U.S. Senate, Washington D.C., October 25, 2001.

Opponents of the Patriot Act have called for its repeal, arguing that it erodes civil liberties while providing minimal security.

Without Any Evidence of Criminal Behavior

Or, to take another change—and thanks to the librarians, more people know about this one—the FBI now has the right to go into any library and ask for the records of everybody who has used the library and get a list of who is reading what. Similarly, the FBI can demand all the records of banks, colleges, hotels, hospitals, credit-card companies, and many more kinds of companies. And these changes are only the beginning. [In November 2003] Attorney

General [John] Ashcroft issued brand new guidelines permitting FBI agents to run credit checks and background checks and gather other information about anyone who is "of investigatory interest,"—meaning anyone the agent thinks is suspicious—without any evidence of criminal behavior.

So, is that fine with everyone? . . .

I have studied the Patriot Act and have found that along with its many excesses, it contains a few needed changes in the law. And it is certainly true that many of the worst abuses of due process and civil liberties that are now occurring are taking place under the color of laws and executive orders other than the Patriot Act.

Nevertheless, I believe the Patriot Act has turned out to be, on balance, a terrible mistake. . . . Therefore, I believe strongly that the few good features of this law should be passed again in a new, smaller law—but that the Patriot Act must be repealed.

Analyze the essay:

1. Despite the fact that he is arguing against the Patriot Act, Gore makes a point of acknowledging that the act contains certain tools that do help law enforcement fight terrorism. Why do you think he makes this concession? What effect does it have on his argument?

2. In this essay Gore complains that the FBI has the power to access a person's library records. In the following essay James D. Zirin argues that knowing what books have been checked out could alert officials to a person's intent to commit terrorism. What do you think? Should the government be able to view personal records such as library records, e-mail, or phone bills for traces of terrorist activity? Why or why not?

The Patriot Act Does Not Reduce Freedom

James D. Zirin

James D. Zirin is a lawyer who practices in New York. In the following essay he argues that the Patriot Act ensures Americans' security without curtailing their freedom. He explains that even though the Patriot Act allows the government greater access to the personal lives of Americans, the law contains checks and balances that prevent it from abusing this power. He views the Patriot Act as reasonable and useful legislation that does not disturb the liberties of Americans in any significant way.

Consider the following questions:

1. What are National Security Letters?
2. How many people has the Justice Department convicted of criminal offenses under the Patriot Act since 2001, according to Zirin?
3. According to the author, how does the Patriot Act compare to the acts of Abraham Lincoln, Franklin Roosevelt, and Hugo Black?

The Patriot Act, overwhelmingly passed by Congress after September 11, 2001, alarms the American Civil Liberties Union, the *Washington Post*, the *New York Times*, government officials in 152 communities, and three states that have passed resolutions condemning this emergency measure.

To these critics, the bill smells of a George Bush plan to undermine civil liberties. . . .

James D. Zirin, "Fearful Patriot Act?" *The Washington Times*, October 22, 2004, p. A18.
Copyright © 2004 by News World Communications, Inc. Reproduced by permission.

Patriot Act Paranoia

A closer examination of facts suggests the paranoia is unjustified. Most of the Patriot Act is devoted to improving information-sharing between the intelligence services and law enforcement. The anti–Patriot Act hysteria stems from a few provisions that merely fine-tune investigative powers granted the government under pre-existing law. The never-used library provisions extend FBI power for warrantless records searches without judicial scrutiny—even on people not themselves terror suspects. The "sneak and peek" provisions authorize the FBI after obtaining a warrant to secretly search homes, cars or offices of anyone, provided the investigation relates to terrorism. The significant change is the search is kept secret. Only law enforcement knows of it.

But is this so horrible? Remember, we are at war. If someone starts reading cookbooks on how to build a dirty bomb, isn't this something the authorities should look into? As for sneak-and-peek, it must be authorized by a federal judge satisfied the authorities have reason to suspect terrorism.

President Bush defends the Patriot Act before an audience of law enforcement officers in 2005, claiming the act is responsible for the capture of more than 200 terrorists.

In other words, the streamlined investigative provisions make it simpler for FBI agents to obtain from phone companies, Internet service providers and other communications companies relevant information, such as e-mail subject lines and cell phone logs, that might foil a terrorist plot. But even these can be used only after getting administrative subpoe-

The Patriot Act allows authorities to monitor the reading selections of library patrons, a provision that has stirred a great deal of controversy.

nas known as National Security Letters. The Act bars recipients of the letters from disclosing to their customers or anyone else that the government scrutinized the records. This prevents alerting terrorists that they are under inquiry. It also guarantees protection of innocent persons' privacy.

We Are at War

Already the Act seems to be producing results. Since 2001, the Justice Department says, as a result of terrorism investigations, it has charged at least 310 defendants with criminal offenses, 179 of whom have been convicted. Many fewer terrorists are on the loose, thanks in part to the Act. Results like this help explain why dedicated public servants like former New York Mayors Rudolph Giuliani and Ed Koch, ex-CIA director James Woolsey and 66 other prominent citizens have written congressional leaders in support of the Act. . . .

A Vital Tool to Target Terrorists

Like the smart bombs, laser-guided missiles and predator drones employed by our armed forces [overseas], the Patriot Act is just as vital to targeting the terrorists who would kill our people and destroy our freedom here at home.

John Ashcroft, address to the U.S. Congress, Washington, DC, July 13, 2004.

So what's all the fuss about anyway? After all, we are at war; and, indeed, the Patriot Act is benign as compared with the deeds of such noted libertarians as Abraham Lincoln, who suspended the writ of habeas corpus during the Civil War, and Franklin Roosevelt, Earl Warren and Hugo Black who authorized the Japanese-American internments during World War II.

A Manhattan federal judge [in September 2004], dealing with a predecessor statute, invalidated Patriot Act procedures for getting information from an Internet service provider. The media were delighted. The *Washington Post* blared, "Key part of Patriot Act ruled unconstitutional." The *New York Times* trumpeted, "Judge strikes down section of the Patriot Act." No such luck. Both papers later admitted they were wrong. Both papers published a "correction" on the Internet the next day. The court decision

Public Opinion About the Patriot Act

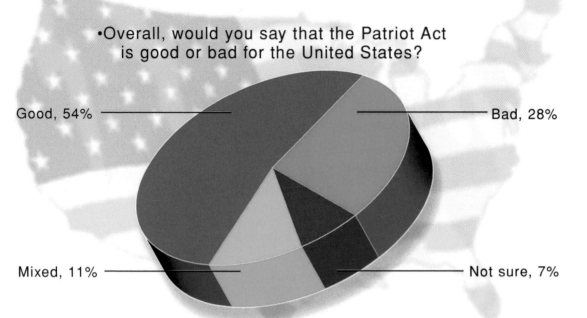

•Overall, would you say that the Patriot Act
is good or bad for the United States?

Good, 54%

Bad, 28%

Mixed, 11%

Not sure, 7%

Source: Fox News/Opinion Dynamics poll, April 2004.

focused not on the Patriot Act, but on the Electronics
Communications Privacy Act of 1986, broadened in 1993
and again by the Patriot Act in 2001.

The Patriot Act Is Reasonable

The knee-jerk reaction of both the *Post* and the *New York
Times* reveals a tendency to fire before they aim or are
ready. Perhaps they see the Patriot Act as a club to bash
[former] Attorney General John Ashcroft. There is much
not to admire in Mr. Ashcroft, but, as the September 11
commission observed: "The choice between security and
liberty is a false choice, as nothing is more likely to endan-
ger America's liberties than the success of a terrorist attack
at home. Our history has shown us that insecurity threatens liberty. Yet if our liberties are curtailed, we lose the
values that we are struggling to defend."

I have read the act carefully, and agree with 99 senators that it is a reasonable way to strengthen intelligence and law enforcement against our sworn enemies while doing no significant damage to traditional liberties.

Analyze the essay:

1. As part of his rationale for why certain provisions of the Patriot Act are reasonable, Zirin reminds his readers, "We are at war." Do you agree or disagree with this idea?

2. Zirin characterizes those who criticize the Patriot Act as having a "knee-jerk reaction" and succumbing to "anti–Patriot Act hysteria." Do you think this is fair? Why or why not?

The Patriot Act Unfairly Targets Immigrants

David Cole

Attorney David Cole is the legal affairs correspondent for the *Nation* magazine and the author of *Enemy Aliens: Double Standards and Constitutional Freedoms in the War on Terrorism*. In the following essay he argues the Patriot Act is anti-immigrant. He gives several examples of immigrants who have been forced to leave the country for exercising their right to free speech and for associating with radical political organizations. Cole argues that people who carry passports from other countries do not deserve fewer rights than Americans and should not be cast out as potential terrorists.

Consider the following questions:

1. According to the author, why was Tariq Ramadan deported?
2. How many foreign nationals have been detained under the Patriot Act, according to Cole?
3. Who is Dora Maria Tellez, and why was she denied entry into the United States?

The Patriot Act debate is on—sort of. Congress has until the end of [2005] to decide whether to reauthorize sixteen "sunsetted" provisions of the act that would otherwise expire on December 31. . . . But if Patriot Act opponents are expecting great things, they will be disappointed. Many of the worst provisions of the act are not even up for discussion. . . . Among the most troubling provisions not sunsetted are those on immigration. They

David Cole, "The Missing Patriot Debate," *The Nation*, May 30, 2005. Copyright © 2005 by The Nation Magazine/The Nation Company, Inc. Reproduced by permission.

authorize the government to deny entry to foreigners because of speech rather than actions, to deport even permanent residents who innocently supported disfavored political groups and to lock up foreign nationals without charges.

Unfair Deportations

Patriot Act proponents often insist that there have been no abuses of the act, but the law's immigration provisions have clearly been abused. In one case, the government ordered an Indian man deported for having set up a tent for religious prayer and food, simply because unnamed members of a "terrorist organization" were allegedly among those who came to services at the tent. In a case I am handling for the Center for Constitutional Rights, the government is seeking to deport two longtime permanent

Kirk. © 2004 by Kirk Anderson. Reproduced by permission.

residents for having distributed PLO [Palestine Liberation Organization] magazines in Los Angeles in the 1980s, and for having organized two Palestinian community dinners at which they raised money for humanitarian causes. The government considers it irrelevant that distributing magazines and raising humanitarian aid was entirely lawful, even constitutionally protected, at the time.

The government has also used the Patriot Act's immigration provisions to revoke the visa of Tariq Ramadan, a Swiss professor and a leading thinker on Islam's relation to modernity. Ramadan, one of the first prominent Muslim scholars to condemn the 9/11 attacks, had been offered a prestigious chair at Notre Dame. Yet the government revoked his visa on the basis of something he said, without ever informing him of what it was. More recently, the government denied a visa to Dora Maria Tellez, a Nicaraguan invited to teach at Harvard, solely because of her association with the Sandinistas [a radical party in Nicaragua] in the 1980s. . . .

Historian Dora Maria Tellez was denied a visa to the United States because of her connection to the Sandinistas, a radical Nicaraguan political party.

Targeting the Vulnerable

So the Patriot Act imposes guilt by association, punishes speech, authorizes the use of secret evidence and allows detention without charges—yet none of that will be subject to the Patriot Act debates. Nor will the debates address the civil liberties abuses committed by US law enforcement agencies or the military outside the Patriot Act—such as the incommunicado detention, without charges or hearings, of hundreds of "enemy combatants" around the world; the use of immigration law to launch a nationwide campaign of ethnic profiling and to detain more than 5,000 foreign nationals, virtually all Arabs or Muslims, none of whom have been convicted of a terrorist crime. . . .

Many of the most pernicious aspects of the Patriot Act, and of the "war on terror" generally, affect foreign nationals exclusively, or nearly exclusively. The act's immigration provisions haven't generated the same concern as the surveillance provisions, not because they are less problematic but because they apply only to "them," not "us."

Thousands of Muslims pray in downtown Cleveland before the opening of a convention focusing on the impact of the Patriot Act on the American Muslim community.

The same is true with respect to practices like torture and rendition, tactics largely reserved for foreign nationals, which have failed to generate the kind of grassroots concern that the libraries provision has. . . .

There is no logical or legal reason why a foreign student living here should have fewer privacy or speech rights than her US citizen classmate. The reason is political—it is always easier to impose such burdens on the most vulnerable. . . .

Rights for All, Not Just Americans

A more promising strategy for the long haul, particularly given the anti-alien character of so many initiatives in the war on terror, would be to emphasize a human rights approach. Human rights, after all, are owed to every person, by virtue of their human dignity, irrespective of the passport they carry. As a strategic matter, human rights campaigns can tap into the power of world opinion and bring it to bear at home, especially when the United States selectively abuses the rights of other countries' nationals.

Analyze the essay:

1. In discussing why immigration policies have not been among the most controversial pieces of the Patriot Act, Cole explains that the laws apply "to 'them,' not 'us.'" How does this idea support the point he makes in the essay?

2. In this essay Cole argues that the Patriot Act unfairly targets immigrants who are not guilty of terrorism. In the following essay author Michelle Malkin argues that the Patriot Act contains reasonable immigration restrictions, considering that America was attacked by foreigners. After reading both essays, with which viewpoint do you agree? What pieces of evidence helped you form your opinion?

The Patriot Act Does Not Target Immigrants

Michelle Malkin

Michelle Malkin is a contributor to *Capitalism Magazine*, from which this viewpoint was taken. In the viewpoint Malkin argues that the Patriot Act contains useful immigration laws that help remove potential terrorists from the country. She claims it has helped fingerprint and arrest many suspected terrorists and prevented others from entering the country. She also points out the drafter of the Patriot Act is himself an immigrant, dispelling myths that the Act is anti-immigrant. Malkin concludes that the United States must be very careful about who comes in and out of the country if it is to avoid another terrorist attack.

Consider the following questions:

1. According to Malkin, how many individuals have been deported from the United States?
2. Who is Viet Dinh?
3. How does Malkin characterize people who compare the Justice Department with the Nazis?

To civil-liberties alarmists, Viet Dinh is a traitor. To me, he is an American hero.

Dinh, 35, is widely known—and reviled—as the primary architect of the Patriot Act. Until May [2003], he was an assistant attorney general for the Office of Legal Policy in [former attorney general] John Ashcroft's Justice Department. (He stepped down to return to his law school post at Georgetown University.) Since the Sept. 11 terrorist attacks,

Michelle Malkin, "Grateful for the Patriot Act," *Capitalism Magazine*, July 3, 2003. *Capitalism Magazine*™ Copyright © 2003 by Bahamas 2003, Ltd. All rights reserved. Reproduced by permission of Michelle Malkin and Creators Syndicate, Inc.

Viet Dinh, a Vietnamese immigrant to the United States, was a principal author of the Patriot Act and he maintains the act is not anti-immigrant.

Dinh told *The Christian Science Monitor,* "our nation's ability to defend itself against terror has been not only my vocation but my obsession."

This Fourth of July holiday, I will give thanks for those like Dinh who have worked tirelessly to ensure domestic tranquility, provide for the common defense, and secure the blessings of liberty that no other country in the world can match.

Enforcing Immigration Laws Fights Terror

A constitutional law expert, Dinh's office had been mostly concerned with judicial nominations before Sept. 11. After the mass murder of 3,000 men, women and children on American soil, Dinh became an instrumental member of the brain trust that designed the Bush administration's anti-terrorism policies. Most importantly, the Patriot Act revised outdated rules that fatally hampered surveillance of suspected terrorists in America. Dinh also helped craft plans to monitor the entry and exit of foreign students and to register and track non-immigrant visitors from high-risk Middle Eastern countries.

An immigrant himself who escaped from communist Vietnam a quarter-century ago aboard a rickety boat, Dinh notes that foreign visitors to our shores are guests obligated to obey the laws—some of which "have not been enforced for 50 years." It was time, Dinh and his colleagues decided, to start enforcing them.

Rafiq Abdus Sabir, a Florida physician, was arrested on terrorism charges as a result of a 2005 sting operation sanctioned by the provisions of the Patriot Act.

The results speak for themselves:

The feds have busted more than 20 suspected al Qaeda cell members from Buffalo, N.Y., to Detroit, Seattle and Portland, Ore.

More than 100 other individuals have been convicted or pled guilty to terrorist related crimes.

The United States has deported 515 individuals linked to the Sept. 11 investigation.

Hundreds of foreign criminals and suspected terrorists, plus one known member of al Qaeda, were prevented from entering the country thanks to the National Entry-Exit Registration System—which Sen. Ted Kennedy attempted to sabotage earlier [in 2003].

Long overdue fingerprint cross checks of immigration and FBI databases at the border have resulted in the arrest of more than 5,000 fugitives, wanted for crimes committed in the United States.

And nearly two years after the Sept. 11 attacks, there has not yet been another mass terrorist attack on our homeland.

The Importance of Borders

As every house has to have a door, every country has to have a border. . . . It is now imperative that we better monitor who we admit into this country.

Richard D. Lamm, "Terrorism and Immigration: We Need a Border," *Vital Speeches of the Day*, March 1, 2002.

Anti-Immigration Claims Are Untrue

Opponents of the Bush administration's homeland defense and immigration enforcement efforts complain that the war on terror has eviscerated civil liberties and constitutional rights. They have falsely portrayed the Patriot Act as allowing the feds to spy on library patrons without a warrant or criminal suspicion—a lie perpetuated by the truth-challenged *New York Times*. They have hysterically compared the detention of illegal aliens from terror-friendly countries to the World War II internment of Japanese. And they have likened Ashcroft, Dinh, and the Justice Department to the Taliban and Nazis. Never mind that the courts have so far upheld every major initiative and tactic from keeping immigration deportation hearings closed, to maintaining secrecy of the names of illegal alien detainees, to allowing use of the Patriot Act surveillance powers.

Dinh is refreshingly unapologetic and to the point in response to the alarmists: "The threat to liberty comes from Osama bin Laden and his terrorist network, not from the men and women in blue who work to uphold the law." Drawing on Edmund Burke's theory of "Ordered Liberty," which argues that liberty cannot be exercised unless government has first provided civil order, Dinh observes: "I think security exists for liberty to flourish and liberty cannot exist without order and security."

This finger-print identification computer software helps immigration inspectors along the U.S.-Mexico border to apprehend fugitives wanted by the FBI.

On July 4th, this fundamental lesson of Sept. 11 must not be forgotten. The charred earth, mangled steel, crashing glass, fiery chaos and eviscerated bodies are indelible reminders that the blessings of liberty in America do not secure themselves.

Analyze the essay:

1. Immigration has always been an important part of America's history. Patriot Act supporters such as Malkin claim the Patriot Act keeps America safe without degrading its commitment to immigration. Patriot Act opponents, such as Cole in the previous essay, argue it is un-American to draft laws that target immigrants. In your opinion, what is the appropriate balance between national security and immigration?

2. Malkin closes her essay with a very vivid description of the terrorist attacks of September 11. Why do you think she chooses to close her essay in this way? How do you think it helps make her point?

THE PATRIOT ACT

IS NOT

ATRIOTIC ACTIO

Section
Two: Model
Essays and
Writing
Exercises

The Five-Paragraph Essay

An essay is a short piece of writing that discusses or analyzes one topic. The five-paragraph essay is a form commonly used in school assignments and tests. Every five-paragraph essay begins with an introduction, ends with a conclusion, and features three supporting paragraphs in the middle.

The Thesis Statement. The introduction includes the essay's thesis statement. The thesis statement presents the argument or point the author is trying to make about the topic. The essays in this book all have different thesis statements because they are making different arguments about the Patriot Act.

The thesis statement should be a clear statement that tells the reader what the essay will be about. A focused thesis statement helps determine what will be in the essay; the subsequent paragraphs are spent developing and supporting its argument.

The Introduction. In addition to presenting the thesis statement, a well-written introductory paragraph captures the attention of the reader and explains why the topic being explored is important. It may provide the reader with background information on the subject matter or feature an anecdote that illustrates a point relevant to the topic. It could also present startling information that clarifies the point of the essay or present a contradictory position that the essay will refute. Further techniques for writing an introduction are found later in this section.

The Supporting Paragraphs. The introduction is followed by three (or more) supporting paragraphs. These are the main body of the essay. Each paragraph presents and develops a subtopic that supports the essay's thesis statement. Each subtopic is then supported with its own facts, details, and examples. The writer can use various kinds of supporting material and details to back up the topic of each supporting paragraph. These may include statistics, quotations from people with special knowledge or expertise, historic facts, and anecdotes. A rule of writing is that specific and concrete examples are more convincing than vague, general, or unsupported assertions.

The Conclusion. The conclusion is the paragraph that closes the essay. Its function is to summarize or reiterate the main idea of the essay. It may recall an idea from the introduction or briefly examine the larger implications of the thesis. Because the conclusion is also the last chance a writer has to make an impression on the reader, it is important that it not simply repeat what has been presented elsewhere in the essay but close it in a clear, final, and memorable way.

Although the order of the essay's component paragraphs is important, they do not have to be written in that order. Some writers like to decide on a thesis and write the introductory paragraph first. Other writers like to focus first on the body of the essay and write the introduction and conclusion later.

Pitfalls to Avoid

When writing essays about controversial issues such as the Patriot Act, it is important to remember that disputes over the material are common precisely because there are many different perspectives. Remember to state your arguments in careful and measured terms. Evaluate your topic fairly—avoid overstating negative qualities of one perspective or understating positive qualities of another. Use examples, facts, and details to support any assertions you make.

The Expository Essay

The previous section of this book provides samples of writings on the Patriot Act. All make arguments or advocate a particular position on the Patriot Act. All include elements of expository writing as well. The purpose of expository writing is to inform the reader about a particular subject. Sometimes a writer will use exposition to simply communicate knowledge; other times, he or she will use exposition to persuade a reader to accept a particular point of view.

Types of Expository Writing

There are several different types of expository writing: definition, classification, process, illustration, and problem/solution. Examples of these types can be found in the viewpoints in the preceding section. The list below provides some ideas on how exposition could be organized and presented. Each type of writing can be used separately or in combination in five-paragraph essays.

Definition. Definition simply tells what something is. Definitions can be encompassed in a sentence or paragraph. At other times, definitions may take a paragraph or more. Defining some topics—especially abstract concepts—can sometimes serve as the focus of an entire essay. For example, in Viewpoint Three, Al Gore's speech mainly defines several provisions of the Patriot Act; through these definitions he makes clear his opinion of them.

Classification. A classification essay describes and clarifies relationships between things by placing them in different categories, based on their similarities and differences. This can be a good way of organizing and presenting information.

Process. A process essay looks at how something is done. The writer presents events or steps in a chronological or ordered sequence of steps. Process writing can either inform the reader of a past event or process by which something was made, or instruct the reader on how to do something.

Illustration. Illustration is one of the simplest and most common patterns of expository writing. Simply put, it explains by giving specific and concrete examples. It is an effective technique for making one's writing both more interesting and more intelligible. For example, Michelle Malkin in Viewpoint Six not only writes in general that the Patriot Act is a useful law, but gives specific examples: at least four terror cells have been broken up in the United States; 515 people have been deported for links to September 11th; and more than five thousand criminal fugitives have been arrested due to new fingerprinting procedures.

Problem/Solution. Problem/solution refers to when the author raises a problem or a question, then uses the rest of the paragraph or essay to answer the question or provide possible resolutions to the problem. It can be an effective way of drawing in the reader while imparting information. James D. Zirin, in Viewpoint Four, identifies as a problem the hysteria and paranoia with which many Americans view the Patriot Act. He then uses his essay to explain why he believes Americans should not be wary of the Patriot Act.

Words and Phrases Common to Expository Essays

Writers use these words and phrases to explain their subjects, to provide transitions between paragraphs, and to summarize key ideas in an essay's concluding paragraph.

accordingly	indeed
because	it is important to understand
clearly	it makes sense to
consequently	it seems as though
first, . . . second, . . . third, . . .	it then follows that
for example	moreover
for this reason	since
from this perspective	subsequently
furthermore	therefore
evidently	this is why
however	thus

America's Controversy: The Patriot Act

Refers to thesis
and topic
sentences

Refers to
supporting
details

Editor's Notes This first model essay is a "defini-tion" expository essay that explains various provisions of the Patriot Act. Each paragraph contains supporting details and information, much of which was taken from resources found in Section One and Section Three of this book. The essay concludes with a paragraph that restates the essay's main idea—that the Patriot Act is one of America's most controversial laws.

As you read this essay, pay attention to its components and how it is organized. Also note that all sources are cited using Modern Language Association (MLA) style. For more information on how to cite your sources see Appendix C. In addition, consider the following questions:

1. How does the introduction engage the reader's attention?
2. What kinds of supporting evidence are used to back up the essay's arguments?
3. What purpose do the essay's quotes serve?
4. How does the author transition from one idea to another?

Paragraph 1

After the September 11 terrorist attacks nearly all Americans agreed that fighting terrorism must become a major priority for the nation. But beyond that basic assessment, opinions quickly divided on how to best approach the problem. Controversy particularly surrounded the Patriot Act, a comprehensive law passed shortly after the attacks. The main purpose of the Patriot Act is to expand federal agents' authority to investigate and prosecute terrorists. Some view the act as critical to capturing terrorists before they strike. To others, the Patriot Act infringes on individual privacy and threatens the civil liberties of all Americans. Despite these strong opinions, most people remain ignorant of what The Patriot Act actually does. Therefore, examining the act's content in detail is critical to determining its role in the war on terrorism.

This is the essay's thesis statement. It determines what the essay will cover.

Paragraph 2

It is important to understand that not all pieces of the Patriot Act are controversial—in fact, the majority of the act's provisions deal with topics that generate little fanfare. For example, the act increases death, cash, and financial benefits for police officers, firefighters, and ambulance and rescue personnel who are disabled or killed in the line of duty. It also provides guidelines for how victims of terrorism should be compensated. Furthermore, the act contains a number of small procedural changes designed to support the war on terrorism. For example, it removes previously existing limits on the amount of money that the government can offer as a reward for information on or capture of terrorists. "Many [of these provisions] have little impact on the daily lives of most Americans," write Ann McFeatters and Karen MacPherson of the *Pittsburgh Post-Gazette*. "For example, the law allows money to be spent to re-establish a government office destroyed by terrorists. It condemns discrimination against Arab or Muslim Americans. It permits the FBI to hire more translators." [1]

This is the topic sentence of the second paragraph.

Transitional phrases such as "furthermore" and "for example" keep the ideas in the essay flowing.

Quote from reputable sources to be sure you use quality information in your essay.

Paragraph 3

The controversy over the Patriot Act is usually limited to less than one-third of the more than one hundred provisions contained within it. One such controversial piece is Section 802, titled "Definition of Domestic Terrorism." This section defines terrorism as "activities that . . . involve acts dangerous to human life." Terrorism is also defined as an act of intimidation to influence the government. Civil libertarians worry that, under a definition this broad, political protesters could be prosecuted as terrorists. As Nancy Chang of the Center for Constitutional Rights explains, "Vigorous protest activities, by their very nature, could be construed as acts that 'appear to be intended . . . to

This is the topic sentence of the third paragraph.

influence the policy of a government by intimidation or coercion.' Further, clashes between demonstrators and police officers and acts of civil disobedience . . . could be construed as 'dangerous to human life' and in 'violation of the criminal laws.'"[2] Supporters of the Patriot Act argue that these concerns are unrealistic. On its Preserving Life and Liberty Web site the Department of Justice states that "peaceful political discourse and dissent is . . . not subject to investigation as domestic terrorism."[3] As of early 2005 no political protestor had been charged under Section 802, but opponents of the Patriot Act remain concerned about its potential for misuse.

Paragraph 4

Another controversial provision is Section 411, which expands the types of offenses for which immigrants may be deported. Section 411 empowers the government to deport immigrants who "engage in terrorist activity." Under Section 411 noncitizens may be deported for being members of, soliciting funds for, or having any type of contact with a terrorist organization. But this includes groups that also serve legitimate political or humanitarian causes. It can be applied even if the immigrant in question has no idea of the organization's terrorist connection. As with Section 802, opponents of the Patriot Act are concerned about such a broad definition of terrorism. Lawyer and author David Cole describes one case in which an Indian man was deported because members of a terrorist organization allegedly visited a tent he set up to distribute food. The American Civil Liberties Union advises that Section 411 "creates a very serious risk that truly innocent individuals could be deported for truly innocent [activities]. . . . Guilt by association is generally forbidden under the First Amendment."[4] But supporters of the act believe that allowing a noncitizen who is even suspected of terrorist ties into the country poses too big a risk to national security. For example, journalist Michelle Malkin regards provisions such as Section 411 to be helping to "secure the blessings of liberty that no other country in the world can match."[5]

Use quotes to back up the points you make. The Nancy Chang quote supports the preceding sentence about the concerns of civil libertarians.

This phrase provides a smooth transition between the two paragraphs.

This information was taken from the David Cole essay in Section One. Collect such information when researching your essay, taking care to express it in your own words.

Use quotes to express impassioned or particularly lively ideas.

Paragraph 5

Section 411 and others like it are prime examples of the tension created between ensuring national security and protecting the rights of individuals. While most of the provisions are accepted as good law enforcement tools, there are many provisions in the Patriot Act that touch off heated controversy. Perhaps it is most accurate to view the Patriot Act as neither perfect nor terrible, but containing some useful provisions and some worrisome ones. As former vice president Al Gore has put it, the Patriot Act contains "many excesses, [but] also contains a few needed changes in the law."[6]

This is the essay's conclusion.

Notes

1. McFeatters, Ann, and Karen MacPherson. "Patriot Act May See Revisions." *Pittsburgh Post-Gazette* 26 Apr. 2004: A1.

2. Chang, Nancy. "The USA Patriot Act: What's So Patriotic About Trampling the Bill of Rights?" Center for Constitutional Rights Nov. 2001 < www.ccr-ny.org >.

3. "Dispelling the Myths." Preserving Life and Liberty < www.lifeandliberty.gov >.

4. "How the Anti-Terrorism Bill Allows for Detention of People Engaging in Innocent Associational Activity." American Civil Liberties Union 23 Oct. 2001 < www.aclu.org >.

5. Malkin, Michell. "Grateful for the Patriot Act." *Capitalism Magazine* 3 July 2003.

6. Gore, Al, prepared remarks on freedom and security 9 Nov. 2003.

Exercise A: Create an Outline from an Existing Essay

It often helps to create an outline of the five-paragraph essay before you write it. The outline can help you organize the information, arguments, and evidence you have gathered in your research.

For this exercise, create an outline that could have been used to write the preceding essay, "America's Controversy: The Patriot Act." This "reverse engineering" exercise is meant to help familiarize you with how outlines can help classify and arrange information.

To do this you will need to
1. articulate the essay's thesis,
2. pinpoint important pieces of evidence,
3. flag quotes that support the essay's ideas, and
4. identify key points that support the argument.

Part of the outline has already been started to give you an idea of the assignment.

Outline

Write the essay's thesis:

I. Paragraph 2 topic: benign portions of the Patriot Act

A.

B. Removed limits on reward money offered for a terrorist's capture

C.

1. *Pittsburgh Post-Gazette* quote further explains some miscellaneous provisions of the Act

II. Paragraph 3 topic:

    A. Civil libertarians worry about the broad definition of terrorism.

        1. Nancy Chang quote shows concerns that Section 802 could be misapplied

    B.

        1.

III. Paragraph 4 topic:

    A.

        1. David Cole anecdote about the Indian man

        2.

    B. The idea that it is dangerous to risk letting those with any contact with terrorists groups remain in the country

        1.

The Patriot Act Is a Necessary Law Enforcement Tool

Editor's Notes One way of writing an expository essay is to use the problem/solution method. Problem/solution refers to raising a problem or a question, then using the rest of the paragraph or essay to answer the question or provide possible solutions to the problem. The following sample essay uses problem/solution to show how the Patriot Act can be a useful law enforcement tool. The author describes a hypothetical terrorist cell in order to discuss what tools authorities would need to disrupt such a cell. The author then uses the essay's supporting paragraphs to describe each of the ways in which the Patriot Act offers solutions to the problem posed.

This essay differs from the previous essay in that it is persuasive, meaning that it attempts to convince the reader of a particular point of view. Pay attention to the ways in which certain phrases attempt to persuade you of the author's viewpoint.

As you read, keep track of the notes in the margins. They will help you analyze how the essay is organized and how it is written.

Refers to thesis and topic sentences

Refers to supporting details

Paragraph 1

How does the author intend to capture the interest of the reader with the introduction?

Consider the following scenario: A terrorist cell composed of four terrorists, who call themselves the Fearsome Four, plans to strike somewhere in the United States. To avoid detection the terrorists spread out to San Francisco, Seattle, Chicago, and Miami. The terrorists in Seattle and Chicago plan their attack over the phone, while the terrorist in San Francisco communicates with the others via e-mail. Although the San Francisco terrorist has been arrested twice for small crimes by local authorities, the FBI is completely unaware of him. Meanwhile, the terrorist in Miami spends many hours at the local library researching books about how to make deadly weapons from basic household ingredients. Despite the fact that these terrorists have taken great pains to go undetected by authorities, they cannot escape the best terror-fighting tool America has at its disposal: the Patriot Act. Several provisions of the act improve law enforcement's ability to bring a terrorist cell such as the Fearsome Four down before it would be able to strike.

What is the essay's thesis statement?

Paragraph 2

The Patriot Act would enable authorities to expose such a cell. The act allows them to monitor the suspected terrorists' communications. One of the powers granted to authorities is the ability to use "roving wiretaps." This means that instead of obtaining a permit to tap just one phone line, as had been the practice, authorities can tap a multitude of lines. As former White House and Pentagon official Douglas MacKinnon has said, the logic granting this authority is clear: "Terrorists don't use one phone," he said. "They use many. Therefore, a 'roving wiretap' is needed."[1] Similar logic is behind why new investigative powers make fighting terrorism easier for law enforcement officials. They can obtain critical information from phone companies, Internet service providers, and other communications companies. Suspicious e-mail subject lines or cell phone logs of unusual calling activity could help FBI agents track down a terrorist plot before it can be executed.

What is the topic sentence of Paragraph 2?

What authorities are quoted throughout the essay?

This material was taken from the James D. Zirin essay in Section One. Note how the author has expressed the information in her own words to avoid plagiarism.

Paragraph 3

Another way in which the Patriot Act would help dismantle a cell like the Fearsome Four is that it helps law enforcement authorities better communicate with each other. This cross-communication has proved invaluable. The absence of such communication before September 11 allowed for terrorism suspects to go unapprehended. Section 203 of the Patriot Act therefore specifically grants officials the "authority to share criminal investigative information."[2] This provision has led to several successes in the war on

What is the topic sentence of Paragraph 3?

What transitional phrases are used to keep the essay moving?

terror. For example, since 2002 information sharing has allowed authorities to dismantle terror cells in Oregon, New York, and Virginia. Similarly, the Patriot Act's information-sharing tools helped San Diego law enforcement prosecute those involved with an al Qaeda plot to exchange drugs for weapons. These and other arrests have caused law professor Paul Rosenzweig to argue, "These are not trivial successes. They're part of an enormous, ongoing effort to protect America from further terrorist attacks. . . . Every time we successfully use the new tools at our disposal to thwart a terrorist organization, that's a victory."[3]

Paragraph 4

What is the topic sentence of Paragraph 4?

Supporting details and specific examples are provided.

Yet another piece of the Patriot Act that could help law enforcement agencies capture members of a group like the Fearsome Four is Section 215. Popularly known as the "library provision," this section grants law enforcement the authority to access library records and many other kinds of records, such as financial, phone, medical, travel, and even video rental records. These records can be searched without a person's knowledge, provided the government says it is trying to protect against terrorism. If applied to the Fearsome Four, law enforcement could use Section 215 to lead them to the terrorist who was checking out books on making weapons. Although there is concern that Section 215 grants the government too much power, such searches could also reveal critical clues in terror investigations. As

Use quoted material to express opinionated or pointed ideas.

author and lawyer James D. Zirin puts it, "If someone starts reading cookbooks on how to build a dirty bomb, isn't this something the authorities should look into?"[4] Officials such as John Ashcroft, when he was attorney general, have taken pains to reassure Americans that the government is not interested in snooping in the records of ordinary people and will focus just on those who seem to pose a threat to society.

Paragraph 5

In the twenty-first century it seems unfortunately clear that terrorism is a problem that will not be solved quickly. With high technology at their disposal, terrorists have found increasingly clever ways with which to communicate and transport materials and goods. Furthermore, they hide themselves among members of a society that prizes personal privacy, making it extremely difficult to weed them out of the general population. Therefore, America needs the laws offered by the Patriot Act that give authorities the power to stop terrorist cells before they strike.

Identify the essay's conclusion. Note how it is based on observations that were made in the essay.

Notes

1. MacKinnon, Douglas. "The Danger of Complacency: Patriot Act Should Be Renewed." *Washington Times* 6 May 2005.

2. "Sunset Provisions of the Patriot Act." *Issues & Controversies on File* 29 Apr. 2005: 172.

3. Rosenzweig, Paul. "Face Facts: Patriot Act Aids Security, Not Abuse." *Christian Science Monitor* 29 July 2004.

4. Zirin, James D. "Fearful Patriot Act." *Washington Times* 22 Oct. 2004: A14.

Exercise A: Create an Outline from an Existing Essay

As you did for the first model essay in this section, create an outline that could have been used to write "The Patriot Act Is a Necessary Law Enforcement Tool." Be sure to identify the essay's thesis statement, its supporting ideas, and key pieces of evidence that are used.

Exercise B: Create an Outline for an Opposing Expository Essay

For this exercise, your assignment is to find supporting ideas, create an outline, and ultimately write an expository essay that argues a view that opposes that of the second model essay. Using information from Section One and Section Three of this book and your own research, you will write an essay that supports the following thesis statement: The Patriot Act is not a necessary law enforcement tool.

Part I. Brainstorm and collect information.

Before you begin writing you will need to think carefully about what ideas your essay will contain. Coming up with these ideas is a process known as brainstorming. Brainstorming involves jotting down any ideas that might make good material when you finally begin to write.

Begin the brainstorming process by simply asking yourself, in what ways is the Patriot Act an unnecessary or harmful law? Use outside research or the material in Section One and Section Three in this book to come up with at least three arguments. Each one should illustrate why the Patriot Act is not a useful or necessary law.

For each of the ideas you come up with, write down facts or information that support it. These could be:

- Statistical information
- Direct quotations
- Anecdotes of past events

Example Paragraph Topic Sentence: The U.S. already had laws that could help catch terrorists.

- The September 11 terrorists carried weapons that were already illegal on airplanes.
- They were in the country in violation of existing immigration laws.
- They had fake IDs.
- They had illegally learned how to fly aircraft.
- Bob Barr quote from Viewpoint Two: "The government had sufficient lawful power to identify and stop the plotters. It failed to do so."

Sometimes you can develop ideas by critically examining the claims your opponent makes. For example, the model essay explains that the Patriot Act could be used to record the phone calls and inspect the library records of suspected terrorists in order to dismantle their cell. But on what grounds should the government detain someone as a suspected terrorist? Remember from Viewpoint Five in Section One how David Cole describes the deportation of seemingly innocent people such as Ramadan and Tellez, neither of whom are terrorists. Learn to retain information like this that could potentially be used to challenge a particular claim.

Come up with two other points that support your thesis statement.

Part II. Place the information from Part I in outline form.

Part III. Write the arguments in paragraph form.

You now have three arguments that support the paragraph's thesis statement, as well as supporting material. Use the outline to write out your three supporting arguments in paragraph form. Make sure each paragraph has a topic sentence that states the paragraph's thesis clearly and broadly. Then, add supporting sentences that express the facts, quotes, and examples that support the paragraph's thesis. The paragraph may also have a concluding or summary sentence.

Looking and Listening: The Patriot Act's Power to Monitor

■ Refers to thesis
and topic
sentences

□ Refers to
supporting
details

Editor's Notes The expository essay is a good medium for explaining complicated subjects to an audience. The following essay demonstrates such a style by exploring some of the ways in which the Patriot Act has allowed government officials to monitor the public. However, unlike the second of the previous model essays, this essay does not attempt to make a persuasive argument. It concerns itself with laying out information for the reader in a clear and illustrative way.

This essay also differs from the previous model essays in that it is longer than five paragraphs. Many ideas require more paragraphs for adequate development. Moreover, the ability to write a sustained research or position paper is a valuable skill. Learning how to develop a longer piece of writing gives you the tools you will need to advance academically.

As you read, consider the questions posed in the margins. Continue to identify thesis statements, supporting details, transitions, and quotations. Examine the introductory and concluding paragraphs to understand how they give shape to the essay. Finally, evaluate the essay's general structure and assess its overall effectiveness.

Paragraph 1

Before the attacks of September 11, 2001, the FBI had become curious about a man named Zacarias Moussaoui. Moussaoui, they would later learn, was an al Qaeda agent who aided the September 11 hijackers. Moussaoui had aroused suspicions because he had attended a flight school where he inquired about whether cockpit doors could be opened during flight, and because he had spent time in Pakistan, where al Qaeda had recruited many operatives. But because the FBI could not prove that Moussaoui was a threat, they could not

The Moussaoui story is used as a vehicle to introduce the essay topic in an interesting way.

obtain a warrant to search Moussaoui's computer or tap his phone.

Paragraph 2

Indeed, the Fourth Amendment protects people against unreasonable searches and seizures. It allows law enforcement agents to have a search warrant for a suspect only when there is "probable cause"—that is, when it is likely criminal activity is going on. This system is supposed to balance the right of individuals to be free from government snooping against the need for the government to investigate crimes. But "consequently," writes Mark Reibling, author of a book on FBI-CIA relations, "the FBI lost its best chance to learn of Moussaoui's links to the other September 11 conspirators before they could strike."[1] Therefore, a priority of the Patriot Act has been to loosen restrictions on law enforcement agents, making it easier for them to obtain warrants to tap suspects' phones, monitor their e-mail and Internet usage, and search their homes and offices.

What is the essay's thesis statement?

Paragraph 3

Several sections of the Patriot Act specify the types of wiretaps and searches that may now be authorized. For example, Section 214 allows the use of "pen register" and "trap and trace" wiretaps. Pen registers monitor the numbers dialed from a suspect's telephone. Trap and trace devices monitor the source of incoming calls. These are somewhat limited forms of wiretap. When used on phone lines, investigators with a pen register or trap and trace warrant may only monitor the numbers dialed to and from a specific phone; they are not permitted to listen in on conversations.

Where is this paragraph's topic sentence?

Paragraph 4

Section 216 of the Patriot Act allows pen register and trap and trace devices to be used to monitor Internet communications. Indeed, some of the most interesting and controversial provisions in the Patriot Act are those that deal with modern communication technologies such as the Internet. Before the Patriot Act, government surveillance of the Internet was largely unregulated. Therefore, one of the main goals of the Patriot Act drafters was to update federal wiretap laws for the Internet era. Deputy Assistant Attorney General Alice Fisher explains the need for such updated laws: "While terrorists who were plotting against our nation traveled across the globe, carrying laptop computers and using disposable cell phones, federal investigators operated under laws seemingly frozen in an era of telegrams and switchboard operators. . . . The USA PATRIOT Act modernized existing law, and gave investigators crucial new tools."[2]

What authorities are quoted in the essay? What do they add to the discussion?

Paragraph 5

However, one problem with this section is that it is unclear exactly what constitutes Internet surveillance. Section 216 states that these devices may not be used to intercept the "content" of Internet communications—but the Patriot Act does not specify what "content" means. For example, it may mean that investigators can monitor the sender and recipient of an e-mail, but not read the e-mail's content. Or it could mean that if investigators are monitoring a suspect's Web surfing, they can keep track of the sites the suspect visits but not read the contents of those sites. Internet privacy groups such as the Electronic Frontier Foundation (EFF) have repeatedly contacted the Department of Justice (DOJ) requesting answers to questions such as these. In January 2005 EFF sent a letter complaining that "the DOJ has refused to answer the public's very simple question: 'Can the government see what I'm reading on the Web without having to show probable cause?'"[3]

What transitions are used to keep the essay moving?

Paragraph 6

Another way in which the Patriot Act seeks to modernize wiretap and warrant laws is by expanding the scope of the warrants themselves. Prior to the Patriot Act most wiretap warrants could only be issued for a specific phone or computer, and a separate warrant had to be procured for each device that a suspect used. Over the years this has become

Note how this essay does not argue a point or attempt to persuade the reader, but neutrally illustrates its subjects in an attempt to explain the topic.

a bigger problem for investigators, as people increasingly use multiple cell phones and computers in the course of their daily lives.

Paragraph 7

Section 206 of the Patriot Act therefore allows warrants to be issued for "roving wiretaps" that can be applied to any and all communications devices associated with a case. Fisher states that "this new authority allows us to avoid unnecessary cat-and-mouse games with terrorists who are trained to thwart surveillance by rapidly changing hotels or residences, cell phones, and Internet accounts before important meetings or communications."[4] However, civil liberties groups warn that roving wiretaps could result in the government tapping dozens of public phones and computers, potentially violating the privacy and Fourth Amendment rights of other people who use them. They argue that the purpose of the warrant system is to enable a judge to oversee the search and surveillance process. When warrants are issued for multiple phones and computers and used nationwide, these groups believe that abuses are more likely to go unnoticed.

Paragraph 8

Yet another piece of the Patriot Act that expands authorities' ability to monitor suspects is Section 213. This provision allows investigators to conduct what are popularly known as "sneak and peek" searches. Normally, police must attempt to notify a suspect of their intention to search before executing a warrant. But in sneak and peek searches, secret searches of a suspect's home or office are conducted without notifying the person until after the search has been completed. The Department of Justice argues that secret searches are necessary because "in some cases if criminals are tipped off too early to an investigation, they might flee, destroy evidence, intimidate or kill witnesses, cut off contact with associates, or take other action to evade arrest."[5]

The types of searches and wiretaps authorized in the Patriot Act will certainly help investigators, but they may also weaken Americans' Fourth Amendment rights. These provisions of the Patriot Act raise important questions about how to balance individual privacy with the need to investigate terrorism. These questions are so difficult because there clearly *is* a need for the government to be able to invade individuals' privacy in order to apprehend terrorists and ensure public safety. As sociologist Amitai Etzioni writes, the Fourth Amendment "does not state that Congress 'shall make no law allowing search and seizure' or anything remotely like it. It states that there be no *unreasonable* searches."[6] In the war on terror, it is up to the American people, their elected officials, and the courts to determine which antiterrorism measures are reasonable and which are not.

Note how the conclusion returns to the discussion of the Fourth Amendment, a subject introduced at the start of the essay.

Notes

1. Reibling, Mark. "Uncuff the FBI." *OpinionJournal.com* 4 June 2002.

2. Fisher, Alice, testimony before the Senate Judiciary Committee 9 Oct. 2002 < http://judiciary.senate.gov >.

3. "FOIA Request to DOJ Concerning Pen-Trap Surveillance." Electronic Frontier Foundation 13 Jan. 2005 < www.eff.org >.

4. Fisher, testimony.

5. "Dispelling the Myths." Preserving Life & Liberty < www.lifeandliberty.gov >.

6. Etzioni, Amitai. *How Patriotic Is the Patriot Act? Freedom Versus Security in an Age of Terrorism.* New York: Routledge, 2004.

Exercise A: Examining Introductions and Conclusions

Every essay features introductory and concluding paragraphs that are used to frame the main ideas being presented. Along with presenting the essay's thesis statement, well-written introductions should grab the attention of the reader and make clear why the topic being explored is important. The conclusion reiterates the essay's thesis and is also the last chance for the writer to make an impression on the reader. Strong introductions and conclusions can greatly enhance an essay's effect on an audience.

The Introduction

There are several techniques that can be used to craft an introductory paragraph. An essay can start with

- an anecdote: a brief story that illustrates a point relevant to the topic;
- startling information: facts or statistics that elucidate the point of the essay;
- setting up and knocking down a position: a position or claim believed by proponents of one side of a controversy, followed by statements that challenge that claim;
- historical perspective: an example of the way things used to be that leads into a discussion of how or why things work differently now;
- summary information: general introductory information about the topic that feeds into the essay's thesis statement.

1. Reread the introductory paragraphs of the model essays in this section and of the viewpoints in Section One. Identify which of the techniques described above are used in the essays. How do they grab the attention of the reader? Are their thesis statements clearly presented?
2. Write an introduction for the essay you have outlined and partially written in the previous exercise using one of the techniques described above.

The Conclusion

The conclusion brings the essay to a close by summarizing or returning to its main ideas. Good conclusions, however, go beyond simply repeating these ideas. Strong conclusions explore a topic's broader implications and reiterate why it is important to consider. They may frame the essay by returning to an anecdote featured in the opening paragraph. Or they may close with a quotation or refer to an event in the essay. In opinionated essays, the conclusion can reiterate which side the essay is taking or ask the reader to reconsider a previously held position on the subject.

1. Reread the concluding paragraphs of the model essays in this section and of the viewpoints in Section One. Which were most effective in driving their arguments home to the reader? What sorts of techniques did they use to do this? Did they appeal emotionally to the reader, or book-end an idea or event referenced elsewhere in the essay?

2. Write a conclusion for the essay you have outlined and partially written in the previous exercise using one of the techniques described above.

Author's Checklist

✔ Review the five-paragraph essay you wrote.

✔ Make sure it has a clear introduction that draws the reader in and contains a thesis statement that concisely expresses what your essay is about.

✔ Evaluate the paragraphs and make sure they each have clear topic sentences that are well supported by interesting and relevant details.

✔ Check that you have used compelling and authoritative quotes to enliven the essay.

✔ Finally, be sure you have a solid conclusion that uses one of the techniques presented in this exercise.

Exercise B: Using Quotations to Enliven Your Essay

No essay is complete without quotations. Get in the habit of using quotes to support at least some of the ideas in your essays. Quotes do not need to appear in every paragraph but should appear often enough so that the essay contains voices aside from your own. When you write, use quotations to accomplish the following:

- provide expert advice that you are not necessarily in the position to know about
- add interest with lively or passionate passages
- include a particularly well-written point that gets to the heart of the matter
- supply statistics or facts that have been derived from someone's research
- deliver anecdotes that illustrate the point you are trying to make.
- express first-person testimony

Now reread the essays presented in the first two sections of this book and find at least one example of each of the above quotation types.

There are a few important things to remember when using quotations:

- Note your sources' qualifications and biases. This way your reader can identify the person you have quoted and can put their words in context.
- Put any quoted material within proper quotation marks. Failing to attribute quotes to their authors constitutes plagiarism, which is when an author takes someone else's words or ideas and presents them as his or her own. Plagiarism is a very serious ethical infraction and must be avoided at all costs.

Write Your Own Expository Five-Paragraph Essay

Using the material in this book, write your own five-paragraph expository essay that deals with the Patriot Act. The following steps are suggestions on how to get started.

Step One: Choose your topic.
Think carefully before deciding on the topic of your essay. Is there any aspect of the Patriot Act that particularly fascinates you? Is there an issue you strongly support or feel strongly against? Is there a topic you would like to learn more about? Ask yourself such questions before selecting your essay topic. Refer to Appendix C: Sample Essay Topics if you need help selecting a topic.

Step Two: Write down questions and answers about the topic.
Recall from Exercise B after Essay Two the process known as brainstorming, in which you ask yourself questions and come up with ideas to discuss in your essay. Possible questions that will help you with the brainstorming process include:

- Why is this topic important?
- Why should people be interested in this topic?
- How can I make this essay interesting to the reader?
- What question am I going to address in this paragraph or essay?
- What facts, ideas, or quotes can I use to support the answer to my question?
- Will the question's answer reveal a preference for one subject over another?

Questions especially for expository essays include:

- Do I want to write an informative essay or an opinionated essay?
- Will I need to explain a process or course of action?
- Will my essay contain many definitions or explanations?
- Is there a particular problem that needs to be solved?

Step Three: Gather facts and ideas related to your topic.
This book contains several places to find information, including the viewpoints and the appendixes. In addition, you may want to research the books, articles, and Web sites listed in Section Three, or do additional research in your local library.

Step Four: Develop a workable thesis statement.
Use what you have written down in numbers 2 and 3 above to help you articulate the main point or argument you want to make in your essay. It should be expressed in a clear sentence and make an arguable or supportable point.

Examples:

Americans who view the Patriot Act with hysteria and paranoia are misguided.

> This could be the thesis statement of an opinionated expository essay that argues that the frenzy over the Patriot Act stems from misinformation about it. It could also discuss the point of view that the invasions of privacy the Patriot Act allows are not such a big deal.

The way the Patriot Act has defined terrorism has caused some confusion and controversy.

> This could be the thesis statement of an informative expository essay that explores how the Patriot Act defines terrorism, what implications the definition has for various provisions, and how Americans have reacted to such a definition.

Step Five: Write an outline or diagram.
 a. Write the thesis statement at the top of the outline.
 b. Write roman numerals I, II, and III on the left side of the page with A, B, and C under each numeral.
 c. Next to each roman numeral, write down the best ideas you came up with in number 3 above. These should all directly relate to and support the thesis statement.
 d. Under each roman numeral, list *a, b,* and *c.* Next to each letter write down information that supports that particular idea.

Step Six: Write the three supporting paragraphs.
Use your outline to write the three supporting paragraphs. Write down the main idea of each paragraph in sentence form. Do the same thing for the supporting points of information. Each sentence should support the paragraph's topic. Be sure you have relevant and interesting details, facts, and quotes. Use transitions when you move from idea to idea to keep the progression of thought fluid and smooth. Sometimes, although not always, paragraphs can include a concluding or summary sentence that restates the paragraph's argument.

Step Seven: Write the introduction and conclusion.
See Exercise A of Essay Three for information on writing introductions and conclusions.

Step Eight: Read and rewrite.
As you read, check your essay for the following:

- Does the essay maintain a consistent tone?

- Do all sentences serve to reinforce your general thesis or your paragraph topics?

- Do all paragraphs flow from one to the other? Do you need to add transition words or phrases?

- Have you quoted from reliable, authoritative, and interesting sources?

- Is there a sense of progression throughout the essay?

- Does the essay get bogged down in too much detail or irrelevant material?

- Does your introduction grab the reader's attention?

- Does your conclusion reflect any previously discussed material or give the essay a sense of closure?

- Are there any spelling or grammatical errors?

Tips on Writing Effective Expository Essays

✔ You do not need to include every detail on your subjects. Focus on the most important ones that support your thesis statement.

✔ Vary your sentence structure; avoid repeating yourself.

✔ Maintain a professional, objective tone of voice. Avoid sounding uncertain or insulting.

✔ Anticipate what the reader's counterarguments may be and answer them.

✔ Use sources that state facts and evidence.

✔ Avoid assumptions or generalizations without evidence.

✔ Aim for clear, fluid, well-written sentences that together make up an essay that is informative, interesting, and memorable.

THE PATRIOT AC
IS NOT
PATRIOTIC ACTI

**Section Three:
Supporting
Research Material**

Facts About the Patriot Act

Editor's Note: These facts can be used in reports or papers to reinforce or add credibility when making important points or claims.

- The official name USA PATRIOT Act of 2001 is an acronym. It stands for Uniting and Strengthening America by Providing Appropriate Tools Required to Intercept and Obstruct Terrorism.
- On October 11, 2001, the act passed 98-1 in the United States Senate. Senator Russell Feingold, a Democrat from Wisconsin, cast the lone dissenting vote.
- On October 12, 2001, the act passed 357-66 in the House of Representatives.
- President George W. Bush signed the act into law on October 26, 2001, forty-five days after the September 11, 2001, attacks.
- In June 2005 Bush said the Patriot Act had helped authorities arrest more than four hundred suspected terrorists. More than half of these arrests resulted in convictions or guilty pleas.
- The Patriot Act is 342 pages long and contains over one hundred provisions. Most of the controversy surrounding the Patriot Act pertains to about sixteen of them.
- Some controversial provisions of the Patriot Act are set to expire in 2006. Congress must vote to decide if these provisions, called "sunset provisions" because they are not permanent, should be renewed or allowed to expire.

Provisions of the Patriot Act Set to Expire

201. Authority to intercept wire, oral, and electronic communications relating to terrorism.
202. Authority to intercept wire, oral, and electronic communications relating to computer fraud and abuse offenses.

203. (b), (d). Authority to share criminal investigative information.
206. Roving surveillance authority under the Foreign Intelligence Surveillance Act (FISA) of 1978.
207. Duration of FISA surveillance of non–United States persons who are agents of a foreign power.
209. Seizure of voice-mail messages pursuant to warrants.
212. Emergency disclosure of electronic communications to protect life and limb.
214. Pen register and trap and trace authority under FISA.
215. Access to records and other items under FISA.
217. Interception of computer trespasser communications.
218. Foreign intelligence information (lowers standard of evidence for FISA warrants).
220. Nationwide service of search warrants for electronic evidence.
223. Civil liability for certain unauthorized disclosures.
225. Immunity for compliance with FISA wiretap.

Permanent Nonexpiring Provisions

203. (a), (c). Authority to share criminal investigative information.
205. Employment of translators by the FBI.
210. Scope of subpoenas for records of electronic communications.
211. Clarification of scope (privacy provisions of Cable Act overridden for communication services offered by cable providers but not for records relating to cable viewing).
213. Authority for delaying notice of the execution of a warrant ("sneak and peek").
216. Modification of authorities relating to use of pen registers and trap and trace devices.

219. Single-jurisdiction search warrants for terrorism.
222. Assistance to law enforcement agencies.

American Attitudes About the Patriot Act

• An August 2003 Gallup poll found that 69 percent of Americans felt the Patriot Act did not go far enough in protecting against terrorism, while 22 percent believed the act went too far. When the same poll was conducted almost two years later in April 2005, only 49 percent of Americans felt the Patriot Act did not go far enough in protecting against terrorism, while 45 percent believed the act went too far.

• An April 2005 Gallup poll asked Americans how much they knew about the Patriot Act. Thirteen percent answered "a lot," 28 percent answered "some," 28 percent answered "not much," and 29 percent answered "nothing."

An August 2005 poll conducted by the Center for Survey Research and Analysis at the University of Connecticut found the following about Americans' attitudes toward the Patriot Act:

"Do you think the Patriot Act has prevented terrorist attacks in the United States?"

Yes	43%
No	44%
Unsure	13%

"Do you think the government should renew the Patriot Act in its current form, renew it with some modifications, or let it expire?"

Renew in Current Form	20%
Renew with Modifications	57%
Let It Expire	17%
Unsure	5%

A July 2005 Fox News/Opinion Dynamics poll asked Americans the following questions regarding the Patriot Act:

"Which do you think is more important: protecting your civil liberties and privacy from being invaded, or protecting your safety and surroundings from terrorism?"

Privacy	43%
Safety	65%
Both	20%
Unsure	2%

"Would you be willing to give up some of your personal freedom in order to reduce the threat of terrorism?"

Yes	64%
No	21%
Unsure	15%

Finding and Using Sources of Information

No matter what type of essay you are writing, it is necessary to find information to support your point of view. You can use sources such as books, magazine articles, newspaper articles, and online articles.

Using Books and Articles

You can find books and articles in a library by using the library's computer or cataloging system. If you are not sure how to use these resources, ask a librarian to help you. You can also use a computer to find many magazine articles and other articles written specifically for the Internet.

You are likely to find a lot more information than you can possibly use in your essay, so your first task is to narrow it down to what is likely to be most usable. Look at book and article titles. Look at book chapter titles, and examine the book's index to see if it contains information on the specific topic you want to write about. (For example, if you want to write about sneak-and-peek searches and you find a book about counterterrorism measures, check the chapter titles and index to be sure it contains information about sneak and peeks before you bother to check out the book.)

For a five-paragraph essay, you do not need a great deal of supporting information, so quickly try to narrow down your materials to a few good books and magazine or Internet articles. You do not need dozens. You might even find that one or two good books or articles contain all the information you need.

You probably do not have time to read an entire book, so find the chapters or sections that relate to your topic, and skim these. When you find useful information, copy it onto a notecard or into a notebook. You should look for supporting facts, statistics, quotations, and examples.

Using the Internet

When you select your supporting information, it is important that you evaluate its source. This is especially important with information you find on the Internet. Because nearly anyone can put information on the Internet, it has as much bad information as good information online. Before using Internet information—or any information—try to determine whether the source seems reliable. Is the author or Internet site sponsored by a legitimate organization? Is it from a government source? Does the author have any special knowledge or training relating to the topic you are looking up? Does the article give any indication of where its information comes from?

Using Your Supporting Information

When you use supporting information from a book, article, interview, or other source, there are three important things to remember:

1. Make it clear whether you are using a direct quotation or a paraphrase. If you copy information directly from your source, you are quoting it. You must put quotation marks around the information and tell where the information comes from. If you put the information in your own words, you are paraphrasing it.

Here is an example of using a quotation:

> Author Jim Cornehls worries that legislation such as the Patriot Act could negatively alter everyday American life. Writes Cornehls: "[Such homeland security] would include national identity cards, surveillance, and subject to search rules in all public places, random searches of vehicles entering airports and parking garages, compiling dossiers on all persons who take scuba diving lessons, tracking the comings and goings of subway riders electronically, and the list goes on and on."[1]

Here is an example of a brief paraphrase of the same passage:

> Author Jim Cornehls worries that legislation such as the Patriot Act could negatively alter everyday American life. He foresees a nation in which everyone is watched, stopped, and searched at all turns. Even seemingly uneventful activities like riding a subway or taking scuba lessons could become subject to government investigation.

2. Use the information fairly. Be careful to use supporting information in the way the author intended it. For example, it is unfair to quote an author as saying, "The Patriot Act is good" when he or she actually said, "The Patriot Act is good at undermining freedom." This is called taking information out of context. Using that information as supporting evidence in that way is unfair.

3. Give credit where credit is due. Giving credit is known as citing. You must use citations when you use someone else's information, but not every piece of supporting information needs a citation.

   - If the supporting information is general knowledge—that is, it can be found in many sources—you do not have to cite your source.
   - If you directly quote a source, you must cite it.
   - If you paraphrase information from a specific source, you must cite it.
   - If you do not use citations where you should, you are plagiarizing—or stealing—someone else's work.

Citing Your Sources

There are a number of ways to cite your sources. Your teacher will probably want you to do it in one of three ways:

   - Informal: As in the examples in number 1 above, tell where you got the information in the same place you use it.

- Informal list: At the end of the article, place an unnumbered list of the sources you used. This tells the reader where, in general, you got your information.
- Formal: Use an endnote as in the first example in number 1. (An endnote is generally placed at the end of an article or essay, although it may be located in different places depending on your teacher's requirements.)

Notes:

1. Cornehls, Jim. "The USA PATRIOT Act: The Assault on Civil Liberties." *Z Magazine* July 2003.

Using MLA Style to Create a Works Cited List

You will probably need to create a list of works cited for your paper. These include materials that you quoted from, relied heavily on, or consulted to write your paper. There are several different ways to structure these references. The following examples are based on Modern Language Association (MLA) style, one of the major citation styles used by writers.

Book Entries

For most book entries you will need the author's name, the book's title, where it was published, what company published it, and the year it was published. This information is usually found on the inside of the book. Variations on book entries include the following:

A book by a single author:
> Guest, Emma. *Children of AIDS: Africa's Orphan Crisis*. London: Sterling, 2003.

Two or more books by the same author:
> Friedman, Thomas L. *From Beirut to Jerusalem*. New York: Doubleday, 1989.
> ———. *The World Is Flat: A Brief History of the Twentieth Century*. New York: Farrar, Straus and Giroux, 2005.

A book by two or more authors:
> Pojman, Louis P., and Jeffrey Reiman. *The Death Penalty: For and Against*. Lanham, MD: Rowman & Littlefield, 1998.

A book with an editor:
> Friedman, Lauri S., ed. *At Issue: What Motivates Suicide Bombers?* San Diego, CA: Greenhaven, 2004.

Periodical and Newspaper Entries

Entries for sources found in periodicals and newspapers are cited a bit differently from books. For one, these sources usually have a title and a publication name. They also may have specific dates and page numbers. Unlike book entries, you do not need to list where newspapers or periodicals are published or what company publishes them.

An article from a periodical:
> Snow, Keith Harmon. "State Terror in Ethiopia." *Z Magazine* June 2004: 33–35.

An unsigned article from a periodical:
> "Broadcast Decency Rules." *Issues & Controversies On File* 30 Apr. 2004.

An article from a newspaper:
> Constantino, Rebecca. "Fostering Love, Respecting Race." *Los Angeles Times* 14 Dec. 2002: B17.

Internet Sources

To document a source you found online, try to provide as much information on it as possible, including the author's name, the title of the document, date of publication or of last revision, the URL, and your date of access.

A Web source:
> Shyovitz, David. "The History and Development of Yiddish." Jewish Virtual Library 30 May 2005 < http://www.jewishvirtuallibrary.org/jsource/ History/yiddish.html > .

Your teacher will tell you exactly how information should be cited in your essay. Generally, the very least information needed is the original author's name and the name of the article or other publication.

Be sure you know exactly what information your teacher requires before you start looking for your supporting information so that you know what information to include with your notes.

Sample Essay Topics

Exploring Three Key Provisions of the Patriot Act

The Patriot Act Makes America Safer

The Patriot Act Does Not Make America Safer

The Patriot Act Threatens Americans' Freedom

The Patriot Act Protects Americans' Freedom

Civil Liberties and the Patriot Act: Exploring the Debate

The Patriot Act Violates Civil Liberties

The Patriot Act Does Not Violate Civil Liberties

The Patriot Act Was Passed Too Hastily

The Patriot Act Is Unfair to Immigrants

Patriot Act Immigration Laws Keep America Safe

Examining the Patriot Act's Stance on Immigration

The Patriot Act's Definition of Terrorism: Reasonable or Unreasonable?

How the Patriot Act Affects Terrorist Financing

Does the Patriot Act Threaten Internet Privacy?

Americans Are Hysterical over the Patriot Act

Americans Should Be Wary of the Patriot Act

The Patriot Act and Library Patron Privacy

The Patriot Act Should Be Expanded

The Patriot Act Should Be Repealed

The Patriot Act's Sneak and Peek Provision: Important or Invasive?

How to Balance Security and Liberty

Organizations to Contact

American Civil Liberties Union (ACLU)
125 Broad St., 18th Fl., New York, NY 10004-2400
(212) 549-2500 • e-mail: aclu@aclu.org
Web site: www.aclu.org

The American Civil Liberties Union is a national organization that works to defend the civil rights guaranteed by the U.S. Constitution. It believes that measures to protect national security should not compromise fundamental civil liberties.

American Enterprise Institute (AEI)
1150 Seventeenth St. NW, Washington, DC 20036
(202) 862-5800 • Web site: www.aei.org

The American Enterprise Institute for Public Policy Research is a scholarly research institute that is dedicated to preserving limited government, private enterprise, and a strong foreign policy and national defense.

CATO Institute
1000 Massachusetts Ave. NW, Washington, DC 20001-5403
(202) 842-0200 • e-mail: cato@cato.org
Web site: www. cato.org

The institute is a nonpartisan public policy research foundation dedicated to limiting the role of government and protecting individual liberties.

Center for Immigration Studies
1522 K St. NW, Suite 820, Washington, DC 20005-1202
(202) 466-8185 • e-mail: center@cis.org
Web site: www.cis.org

The Center for Immigration Studies is the nation's only think tank dedicated to research on and analysis of the economic, social, and demographic impacts of immigration on the United States. The center supports immigration policy that is both pro-immigrant and restrictive.

Council on American-Islamic Relations (CAIR)
453 New Jersey Ave. SE, Washington, DC 20003
(202) 488-8787 • e-mail: cair@cair-net.org
Web site: www.cair-net.org

CAIR is a nonprofit organization that challenges stereotypes of Islam and Muslims and offers an Islamic perspective on public policy issues.

Electronic Frontier Foundation (EFF)
454 Shotwell St., San Francisco, CA 94110 • (415) 436-9333
e-mail: eff@eff.org • Web site: www.eff.org

EFF is a watchdog organization for the preservation of civil liberties on the Internet. It develops positions on free speech, encryption, privacy, and intellectual property.

Electronic Privacy Information Center (EPIC)
1718 Connecticut Ave. NW, Suite 200, Washington, DC 20009
(202) 483-1140 • Web site: http://epic.org

EPIC was established in 1994 to focus public attention on emerging civil liberties issues and to protect privacy, the First Amendment, and constitutional values.

Federal Bureau of Investigation (FBI)
935 Pennsylvania Ave. NW, Rm. 7972, Washington, DC 20535
(202) 324-3000 • Web-site: www.fbi.gov

The FBI, the principal investigative arm of the U.S. Department of Justice, has the authority and responsibility to investigate specific crimes assigned to it. The FBI also is authorized to provide other law enforcement agencies with cooperative services, such as fingerprint identification, laboratory examinations, and police training.

United States Department of Justice (DOJ)
950 Pennsylvania Ave. NW, Washington, DC 20530-0001
(202) 514-2000 • e-mail: AskDOJ@usdoj.gov
Web site: www.usdoj.gov

The function of the DOJ is to enforce the law and defend the interests of the United States according to the law; to ensure public safety against foreign and domestic threats; to provide federal leadership in preventing and controlling crime; to seek just punishment for those guilty of unlawful behavior; to administer and enforce the nation's immigration laws fairly and effectively; and to ensure fair and impartial administration of justice for all Americans.

Bibliography

Books

Ball, Howard, *The USA Patriot Act: Balancing Civil Liberties and National Security: A Reference Handbook*. Santa Barbara, CA: ABC-CLIO, 2004. Provides an overview of the issues surrounding the Patriot Act as well as other laws that have impacted the war on terrorism.

Cohen, David B., and John W. Wells, eds., *American National Security and Civil Liberties in an Era of Terrorism*. New York: Palgrave Macmillan, 2004. This anthology contains eleven essays on how the war on terror is affecting civil liberties, one of which is focused entirely on the Patriot Act.

Etzioni, Amitai, *How Patriotic Is the Patriot Act? Freedom Versus Security in an Age of Terrorism*. New York: Routledge, 2004. Assesses a variety of national security measures, arguing whether or not each measure is justified.

Kettl, Donald F., *System Under Stress: Homeland Security and American Politics*. Washington, DC: CQ, 2004. Discusses the political difficulties of implementing homeland security measures. One of seven chapters focuses on the Patriot Act.

Leone, Richard C. and Greg Anrig Jr., eds., *The War on Our Freedoms: Civil Liberties in an Age of Terrorism*. New York: PublicAffairs, 2003. Features thirteen essays on civil liberties in the war on terrorism, most of which emphasize the need for checks and balances to prevent abuse by counterterrorism measures.

Periodicals

Barr, Bob, "Patriot Act Problems," *World and I*, October 2004.

Blum, Vanessa, "Pitching the Patriot Act," *Legal Times*, August 2, 2004.

Bonopartis, Nik, "Patriot Act Helps Police in Fighting Crime," *Poughkeepsie (NY) Journal*, September 29, 2003.

Center for Democracy and Technology, "Patriot Act Sunsets," May 7, 2004. www.cdt.org.

Chang, Nancy, "The USA Patriot Act: What's So Patriotic About Trampling the Bill of Rights?" Center for Constitutional Rights, November 2001. www.ccr-ny.org.

Dart, Bob, "Patriot Act Faces Opposition from the Left and Right," *San Diego Union-Tribune*, March 23, 2005.

Electronic Frontier Foundation, "FOIA Request to DOJ Concerning Pen-Trap Surveillance," January 13, 2005. www.eff.org.

McCutcheon, Chuck, "Dispute Looms on Patriot Act Renewals," *New Orleans Times-Picayune*, March 23, 2005.

McFeatters, Ann, and Karen MacPherson, "Patriot Act May See Revisions," *Pittsburgh Post-Gazette*, April 26, 2004.

Mehegan, David, "Literary Groups Decry Patriot Act as Invasion of Privacy," *Boston Globe*, May 16, 2003, p. A6.

Preserving Life and Liberty, "Dispelling the Myths." www.life andliberty.gov.

Reibling, Mark, "Uncuff the FBI," *OpinionJournal.com*, June 4, 2002. www.opinionjournal.com.

Rice, Robin, "The USA Patriot Act and American Libraries," *Information for Social Change*, Winter 2002/2003. www.libr.org.

Siddiqui, Jeff, "Muslims Are Targets of Paranoid U.S.," *Seattle Post-Intelligencer*, May 5, 2005.

Zoller, Martha, "The Patriot Act Is Just Right for America," *World and I*, October 2004.

Speeches and Testimony

Ashcroft, John, "The Proven Tactics in the Fight Against Crime," Washington, DC, September 15, 2003. www.usdoj.gov.

Barr, Bob, testimony before the Senate Judiciary Committee, September 22, 2004. http://judiciary.senate.gov.

Bush, George W., remarks at Kleinshans Music Hall, Buffalo, NY, April 20, 2004. www.whitehouse.gov.

———, remarks on the Patriot Act in Columbus, OH, June 9, 2005. www.whitehouse.gov.

Fisher, Alice, testimony before the Senate Judiciary Committee, October 9, 2002. http://judiciary.senate.gov.

Web Sites

Center for Democracy and Technology (www.cdt.org). The CDT is concerned with constitutional liberties in the digital age. It seeks practical solutions to enhance free expression and privacy in global communications technologies.

Department of Homeland Security (DHS) (www.dhs.gov). Offers a wide variety of information on homeland security, including press releases, speeches, and testimony, and reports on new initiatives in the war on terrorism.

National Immigration Forum (NIF) (www.immigration forum.org). Advocates public policies that welcome immigrants and refugees and that are fair and supportive to newcomers to the United States. The NIF Web site offers a special section on immigration in the wake of September 11.

Patriots to Restore Checks and Balances (www.checks balances.org). An anti–Patriot Act group composed of individuals who believe the act infringes on the rights of law-abiding Americans.

Preserving Life and Liberty (www.lifeandliberty.gov). Set up by the U.S. Department of Justice to address civil libertarians' concerns about the Patriot Act and other homeland security initiatives. Offers answers to frequently asked questions about the Patriot Act and testimony from U.S. officials in support of the act.

Index

American Civil Liberties Union (ACLU), 54
Arnaout, Enaam, 16
Ashcroft, John, 15, 29, 34

Barr, Bob, 19
Black, Hugo, 33
Burke, Edmund, 45

Capitalism Magazine, 40
Chang, Nancy, 53–54
Christian Science Monitor (newspaper), 42
Cole, David, 36, 54

Dinh, Viet, 41–42, 43, 45
domestic terrorism, 53

Electronic Frontier Foundation (EFF), 66
Electronics Communications Privacy Act (1986), 33–34
enemy combatants, 25–26
Etzioni, Amitai, 68

Feingold, Russell, 9
Fisher, Alice, 66
Fourth Amendment, 65, 68
Franklin, Benjamin, 11, 23

Giuliani, Rudolph, 33

Gore, Al, 24, 55

information sharing, 59–60
Internet surveillance, 27, 32, 65–66

Kennedy, Ted, 44
Koch, Ed, 33

MacKinnon, Douglas, 59
MacPherson, Karen, 53
Malkin, Michelle, 41, 54
McFeatters, Ann, 53
Moussaoui, Zacarias, 64

National Security Letters, 32–33
New York Times (newspaper), 33, 44

Ordered Liberty theory, 45

Patriot Act. *See* USA Patriot Act
pen registers, 65
Pittsburgh Post-Gazette (newspaper), 53
public opinion. *See* surveys

Ramadan, Tariq, 38
Reibling, Mark, 65
Reno, Janet, 15

Roosevelt, Franklin D., 33
Rosenzweig, Paul, 13, 60
roving wiretaps, 59, 67

security, liberty vs.,
  9–10, 18, 55
September 11 attacks
  (2001), 7
sneak and peek searches,
  27, 67
  justification of, 31–32
surveys, 9–10, 34

Tellez, Dora Maria, 38
terrorism
  Patriot Act is critical
    tool against, 17–18
  pre-Patriot Act laws
    were adequate to
    fight, 20–21
torture, 40
trap and trace wiretaps,
  65

Twain, Mark, 13

USA Patriot Act (2001),
  7, 15, 22, 53
  immigration provisions
    of, 54
  are fair, 42–43
    con, 37–39
  is critical tool against
    terrorism, 17–18
  con, 20–21
  objections to, 8, 14
  safeguards and, 26,
    33

warrants, 66–67
Warren, Earl, 33
Washington Post
  (newspaper), 33
wiretaps, 59, 65, 67
Woolsey, James, 33

Zirin, James D., 30, 60

Picture Credits

Cover: Spencer Platt/Getty Images
AP/ Wide World Photos, 14, 21, 28, 38, 39, 45
EPA/Gary I. Rothstein/Landov, 43
Getty Images, 10, 31
Landov, 9, 15
Michael Kleinfeld/UPI/Landov, 42
Mike Hvozda/U.S. Coast Guard, 8
© Mike Segar/Reuters/CORBIS, 32
© Mike Simons/CORBIS, 22
Reuters/Landov, 16
© Reuters/CORBIS, 16 (inset)
Roger L. Wollenberg/UPI/Landov, 25
Victor Habbick Visions, 17, 34

About the Editor

Lauri S. Friedman earned her bachelor's degree in religion and political science from Vassar College. Much of her studies there focused on political Islam, and she produced a thesis on the Islamic Revolution in Iran titled *Neither West, Nor East, but Islam*. She also holds a preparatory degree in flute performance from the Manhattan School of Music and is pursuing a master's degree in history at San Diego State University. She has edited more than ten books for Greenhaven Press, including *At Issue: What Motivates Suicide Bombers?*, *At Issue: How Should the United States Treat Prisoners in the War on Terror?*, and *Introducing Issues with Opposing Viewpoints: Terrorism*. She currently lives near the beach in San Diego with her yellow lab, Trucker.